Maybe I'll Be Cleverer Tomorrow

A reflection on a complex and
often prickly father/daughter relationship

Pamela Bradley

BALBOA
PRESS
A DIVISION OF HAY HOUSE

Balboa Press books may be ordered through booksellers or by contacting:

Balboa Press
A Division of Hay House
1663 Liberty Drive
Bloomington, IN 47403
www.balboapress.com.au
1 (877) 407-4847

Print information available on the last page.

ISBN: 978-1-5043-0215-9 (sc)
ISBN: 978-1-5043-0216-6 (e)

Balboa Press rev. date: 05/10/2016

For my sons, Adam, Josh, and Ben; and in memory of my father, who really only ever wanted the best for me.

We each grew up with a whole range of beliefs about ourselves, about life, relationships and more. They were taken on unconsciously as part of the fabric of our family … Each belief adds depth and more colour to the lenses we wear. It's the way we see things. It's what we believe to be true.

—Petrea King, *Your Life Matters*

Contents

Foreword by Alison Whitelock xi

Part 1: Up North 1

1 An XPT to Murwillumbah 3
2 An Old Bomb and a Set of Hot Rollers 13
3 A Sleeping Bag and a Lladro Figurine 21
4 Further Unexpected Surprises 26
5 A Country Pub and Salvador Dali 33
6 Thoughts in a Tweed Valley Cemetery 39
7 Tracksuit and Tucker Time at Tumbulgum 44
8 A Cunning Old Bugger 53
9 A Last Hurrah and a Diminishing World 59
10 Turning Points 67
11 Revelations at Coolangatta Airport 75

Part 2: Down South 81

12 Room 22, South Wing 83
13 Fellow Residents and a Family Day 88
14 A Funny Old Geezer 95
15 If Only I Didn't Have to Go 103
16 An Intriguing Postcard 108
17 I Lived Here Once Long Ago 113

18 A Laundry and a Concrete Slab 120

19 Out the Back, Down the Back, and Inside...... 124

20 A Floppy Blue Hat and a Concert................... 133

21 A Place of Diamond-Bright Days................... 138

22 Oysters and Prawns at a Sutherland Hotel 143

23 Getting Back to Basics.................................... 147

24 Moving On... 153

25 Not Quite Good Enough................................ 158

26 Rearing Its Ugly Head 165

27 A Bridge, a River, and a Lion 170

28 A Bus Trip with Harriet................................ 177

29 One Day I'll Show Him 183

30 A Seventeen-Year-Old Parrot........................ 190

31 The House That Greg Built........................... 195

32 Marriage and Swinging England 202

33 Fishermen and Grandfathers.......................... 208

34 Alcohol and Family Brawls 215

35 Christmas: A Whole Load of Humbug........... 222

36 A Club on the Water and a Dream of a Car
    Accident 229

Part 3: Towards the West 239

37 Departures and Letting Go 241

38 Contemplation at 9,000 Metres 248

39 Still With Me 253

40 The Changing Moods of Praiano 258

41 The Beginning of the End 263

42 A Winter Send-Off.. 271

Foreword

As a fellow writer, I find it a tad difficult to evade the grip of intense envy at Pamela Bradley's thirteenth book, *Maybe I'll Be Cleverer Tomorrow*.

I first met her in a Sydney Harbour–side café years ago when I'd just had my own memoir published and her first was about to hit the shelves. We got on famously and began meeting regularly, often chatting for hours, covering everything from relationships to ancient history, feminism to politics, religion to art. We discovered we had much in common: we both enjoy a glass of South Australian Shiraz and are passionate advocates of fairness, and neither of us can possibly wear a bra while writing.

While reading Pamela's latest memoir, I was reminded of the poet Sharon Olds. Olds's work is known for the ordinariness of her subject matter, and yet her writing about these subjects renders them extraordinary. And so it is with this book: the story of a father and daughter told with insight, hilarity, and tenderness. There are so many intensely emotional moments within it, conveyed with the most delicate of brushstrokes, that I was often moved to tears. These moments have embedded themselves in discrete alcoves of my heart. I doubt they will ever disappear.

Pamela's reflection on her relationship with her dad, told in her distinctive voice, made me reflect on the recent death of my own father, the agonising journey we take as adult children treading the final days of a parent's life, and how we find ourselves examining our past, seeking answers to questions such as: How did we become who we are? How much of our parents' beliefs and values did we take on? And how much of what we appear to be is our pure authentic self? Pamela's story is my story. It is all our stories.

Maybe I'll Be Cleverer Tomorrow reflects her dry wit, her intellect, her insatiable need to question, and what one of her friends described as her 'withering' honesty. To my mind, such honesty is refreshing, for without it we would not have gone on this rich, often hilarious and heartbreaking journey, told with a depth of insight that can only be gained by reaching into the darkest recesses of our souls.

—Alison Whitelock, author of *Poking Seaweed with a Stick and Running Away from the Smell*

Part 1

Up North

1

An XPT to Murwillumbah

Barely a day goes by now when I don't think of the solitary life my elderly father lives Up North—casually sidelined, some might think, by his adult children busy with the distractions of their lives.

But that's not really true.

We didn't sideline him. *He* made a choice.

At an age when many old people move closer to the kids, my tough, independent father did the opposite. A year after the death of my mother ended their marriage of fifty-five years, he left Sydney's south, where he had lived all his adult life, and transplanted himself 900 kilometres Up North. At the time, I was reminded somewhat of Frank, the cantankerous old bugger in David Williamson's classic 1979 play *Travelling North*. But unlike Frank, Dad was travelling alone when he flew to the brash and tinselly resort strip of Surfers Paradise, where he had previously bought several units on the beach and where he and his 'girl' were planning to settle into a gracious retirement. Not only did he distance himself physically, he began to withdraw emotionally from family and friends—everything that reminded him of his previous life.

I often wondered if he felt abandoned by Mum's death, and that brought back into play patterns from his childhood and a determination to survive no matter what. Perhaps he feared the family would somehow diminish him by curbing his independence if he remained Down South. On the other hand, he may have felt a sense of freedom, of release from the duty of looking after her, and – cordoned off from his former social life – seen an opportunity to make a fresh start, to experience something new.

I'm not sure if any of us really knew what motivated him, but he joined the wealthy, ageing couples and glitzy middle-aged widows and divorcees fleeing the bitter winters, memories, and ex-husbands of the southern cities. Surfers Paradise seemed to suit him. He could just pop downstairs to pick up groceries and his newspaper, the nearby bottle shop delivered his weekly order of white wine and Johnnie Walker Scotch, and there were plenty of places within walking distance to have lunch.

That experiment lasted no more than a year. On an impulse, he up and left. He moved to the Tweed Valley town of Murwillumbah in northern NSW, a most un-Dad-like place – one with which he had no former association – and purchased a three-bedroom unit in a retirement village 5 kilometres from the centre of town.

So that's where I'm headed. It's 1998 and my first visit since he moved there.

*

I verify the timetable for the North Coast Rail Service and check my ticket: first class, Carriage C, close to the buffet car. I'm twenty minutes early according to the huge bronze clock suspended over the cavernous 1907 Grand Concourse of Sydney's Central Country Railway Station. The XPT is already waiting at Platform 1, and the hall is slowly filling. Apart from three backpackers and a few homeless men asleep in a corner, the majority of people in the domed hall appear to be what are referred to now as seniors.

My father, no matter how old, would *never* take the train; too slow for him. He is an impatient man, eager to get wherever he is going as quickly as possible. Delays of any kind irritate him.

The elderly pensioners – on one of their two free first-class trips a year – move at a snail's pace towards the far end of the platform, their wheeled luggage thwacking against the tiles. From time to time, one poor old thing has to wrestle to keep his or her case going in the right direction.

I lug my suitcase up the three steps into the carriage, stow it out of the way, and find my seat. On the other side of the aisle, a woman – as frail as a bird and breathing in shallow gulps – sinks into the window seat. A man on a cane, with a gaunt face and a few strands of grey hair, settles gingerly beside her.

There's a commotion at the far end of the carriage as a blue-blazered group block the aisle with their luggage. A robust man with a heavy gold neck chain and dyed black hair issues instructions about the placement of bags. He has a strong accent: Greek, I think. A beefy woman, sun-damaged with bleached hair, also adorned in gold, is speaking on one of the latest Nokia 5100s with a pale blue snap-on cover.

'Oh, for God's sake, Elene, put that thing away,' the man says.

'It's Sophia.'

'Can't you let her be?' he snorts.

She ignores him and continues her last-minute conversation.

A whistle, followed by a series of light clacks and thumps, announces our departure, and the train slithers out of the station. It proceeds slowly for the first few kilometres past a mix of inner-city backyards, some still looking like they did in the 1950s – *slums*, we used to call them when I was a child – and others recently gentrified. Members of the group are still dithering, some swapping seats and teetering in the aisle. As we approach Strathfield station, Con, the organiser, hangs out of the door searching for more of the blue blazers.

A bald bloke clutching a takeaway coffee that spills as the train jerks forward falls into the remaining seat beside me. He reeks of cigarettes. 'Hi,' I say. He barely nods. This is not going to be good.

A sweet sickly perfume hangs in the air. I'd take a guess at Elene. She and her friends have settled in the seats behind me, gossiping and giggling like a bunch of schoolgirls on an excursion. The men, who have occupied the area closest to the buffet car, pull out packs of cards and deposit little piles of money in front of them, the whole scene reminiscent of the back room of a taverna in Athens, minus the ouzo and the blue clouds of cigarette smoke.

Before we've even left the metropolitan area, the man beside me is up. He's restless – flexing, stretching, and pacing the aisle as if he's on a bloody plane. A corporate-suited fifty-something woman opposite is absorbed in highlighting pages of text. She barely raises her head.

The train rattles over the Hawkesbury River Bridge and picks up speed through the rugged sandstone landscape of cuttings and tunnels. The frail old couple have already been lulled into sleep by the click-clacking rhythm of the wheels, and the chatter behind me strays from bowling to grandchildren. I need a coffee and swing down the aisle towards the buffet car, passing the men absorbed in their card game.

'How far are you guys going?' I ask.

'Grafton. To a bowling tournament.'

'Sounds like fun,' I say, but I don't mean it.

On my return, balancing a cardboard tray with coffee and a stodgy doorstopper of a railway muffin, the women's conversation has toned down somewhat.

'Maria's such a good daughter. Visits every day.'

Her words thrum in my ears.

'… married forty years … not coping with her grief at all.'

And I wonder if men adjust to their losses more easily than women even when they've been happily married for a long time.

*

After Mum's death but before he moved Up North, my father was living alone in his Sydney unit in the CBD. I had caught the bus in from Balmain to check if he was okay. He must have seen me through his peephole, for he answered the door in his singlet and underpants. 'Hi darl. Can't stop for long. I'm off to the Eastern Suburbs.'

'So what's in the Eastern Suburbs, Dad?'

'Just something new I want to check out,' he said and disappeared to get dressed.

In the daily paper, left open on the dining table, was a circled advertisement urging men suffering erectile dysfunction to contact a clinic in Bondi Junction. I'm somewhat shocked, but then I remember: 'My girl and I know all that sexy stuff,' he used to say, trying to impress us.

Did I now expect him to forsake all that 'sexy stuff' until he died?

He reappeared from the bedroom all dressed up, walked over to the newspaper, and folded it in two.

'Do you miss Mum terribly?' I asked. I had been somewhere in the air on my way home from Egypt when she died. A 'sudden cerebrovascular accident', the death certificate said. I never said goodbye to her.

'What the bloody hell do you think?' he snapped. 'Are you a complete dill?'

'It's just that …'

'You think I'm not grieving enough, is that it?'

'No … not really,' I lied.

'I did most of my grieving in bed beside her when I found she'd gone.'

'I'm sorry. Just worried about you, Dad.'

'Well, don't be. We all have to die. What do you want me to do? I've got to go on.'

'But you're still vulnerable right now.'

'Come on, get out; I need to lock up. Don't waste your bloody time worrying about me.'

*

The train windows rattle as a southbound XPT whooshes past. The landscape has changed to lush rolling hills, sunlight highlighting their contours. I catch my reflection in the dusty window, and for a brief moment see something of my father in my own facial contours. Lately I've come to acknowledge other similarities, like my 'withering' honesty, pointed out by a friend. Or was it 'brutal'? I can't really remember the context of her backhanded compliment. And then there's our rather similar scathing humour. I suspect I'm becoming much more like Dad as I age, and it's an unsettling revelation.

Three and a half hours after we leave Sydney, we rumble into the station of the small Hunter Valley town of Dungog. The twitchy man beside me, carrying only a small overnight bag and taking his foul stench with him, is already striding to the carriage door – anxious, I suspect, to light up. The professional woman opposite is still absorbed in her editing, underlining with a yellow marker pen.

I focus on the purr and gentle rumble of the train, noting the periodic clack of wheels on joints in the track, counting to see if there's a pattern. The old bloke on the other side of the aisle has woken himself up with a barking cough, but his wife doesn't stir. A heavily built XPT employee moves through the carriage taking orders and payment for hot lunches: 'A juicy Chicken Maryland or lovely Beef and Vegetable Casserole,' he calls. The bowlers opt for the cooked meal; I decline, and the old man shakes his head. He turns to me and says, 'We brought our own ham sandwiches with us.'

'Sensible of you,' I say. 'Where are you off to?'

'Home to Urunga. We've been in Sydney to a specialist. My sister has a problem with her heart.'

His sister! 'So you look after her?'

'That's the way it goes, love.'

'She's lucky to have family to care for her.'

'Just the two of us left now.'

'It must be tough on you,' I say.

He shrugs his bony shoulders. 'That's what families do, isn't it?' He turns to his sister and touches her arm. 'Grace.'

I look away, and in my mind's eye I see the future: limited family contacts with Dad and the brief obligatory call-ins on the way to somewhere else.

If only I'd spent more time with him over the years, shared more intimate thoughts, got to know how he really felt about things. But he never opened up about his inner feelings to me, only ever about his love for Mum. And most of our conversations as I grew older had somewhat of an edge to them. But maybe it's not too late.

The train wheels squeal as we lurch to a halt in the middle of nowhere. As if this trip isn't bloody long enough!

Thirty minutes later, we begin to crawl haltingly along the track. Someone cheers, and the driver toots at a cluster of workmen gathered on the side of the line as the lunch announcement from the buffet car leads to a mass exodus of bowlers. I wait until they stagger back with their meals before heading to the bar for a wilted salad and a small bottle of Chardonnay. On my return, I hear one of the bowlers complain as he picks through his soggy vegetables, 'It's a bit light on the meat, don't you think?'

At Urunga, the old man and his grey-faced sister leave the train, and from behind me, I hear, 'My sugar's been sky-high again. Just been put onto a new medication, seems to be working, but I have terrible diarrhoea.'

Please … spare me the details.

Another voice: 'Have a look at this.'

'Ah, that's ter … rible.'

'Steroids.'

I'm trying to imagine what is being revealed behind me when another voice chimes in, 'Decided to have the veins in my left leg stripped later in the year.'

For the next half hour or so, I'm subjected to a series of horror stories about haemorrhoids and colonoscopies, removal of centimetres of lower intestine, streptococcus caught during a hospital stay, and mammograms and mastectomies. Why is it that for many older people, medical conditions become the primary preoccupation?

I make my way once again to the buffet car, countering the swaying motion of the train and gulping down two more small plastic glasses of wine.

At Coffs Harbour, the professional woman departs with her manuscripts or annual company reports or … whatever. How would I know? She initiated no conversation the entire way from Sydney. I fit headphones into my ears and, as the train negotiates the series of Red Hill Tunnels, slip my tape of Don McLean's 1970s *American Pie* into my tape recorder.

I must have drifted off, for I am awakened by a flurry of activity. My head is throbbing – bloody cheap wine! Bags are being pushed and pulled towards the door. We have reached Grafton, where the blue-blazer brigade alight. I rewind the tape and play McLean's moving 'Starry Starry Night' as the train rumbles on to Casino, after which it crosses the tableland and descends through the lush hinterland hills towards the coast. It's dark by the time we pass through the villages of Bangalow, Byron Bay, Mooball, and Burringbar to our final destination of Murwillumbah, almost two hours late.

I wonder if he'll be there, as it's well past his normal bedtime and he's bound to be pissed off at the delay.

2

An Old Bomb and
a Set of Hot Rollers

The train rolls slowly into the platform, and there he is – the man who for over four decades I have thought of as tough and critical, a man who could impale me with a few carefully chosen words. As I alight and walk towards him, I wonder what the hell the next few days will bring.

He looks up, smiles, and announces to a middle-aged woman standing beside him, 'My eldest offspring.'

'Who was she?' I ask when we reach the car park.

'Don't have a bloody clue,' he says, heading towards a beat-up old bomb that looks like something from the early 1980s. Surely that doesn't belong to him. What the hell can he have been thinking?

He throws my bag into the boot, gives the passenger-side door a few jiggles followed by a firm tug, and helps me in. The car smells of body odour and stale car freshener. He starts it up. There's a crunch and a knock as he puts it in first gear and does a teenage-like half wheelie in the slowly emptying car park. By the light of the dashboard, I catch him grinning as he moves out into the dimly lit road that leads into town.

What happened to the man who prided himself on a perfectly functioning machine and the purr of a well-maintained motor, the man who'd power along the highway with his head stuck out the car window listening for an elusive click or ping, never giving up until he found it? Of course, these days his hearing is bad, the price of working on the factory floor among his men for all those years – but surely a partly deaf old mechanical engineer would still be able to *feel* when something wasn't quite right.

I search around for the seat belt. 'Don't bother,' he says. 'There aren't any.'

Once we are in the relative emptiness of Wollumbin Street, he pushes his foot down on the accelerator, and I brace myself for some mishap, my left arm ready to fend off the occasional parked car as we skim dangerously close. My right arm rests on the dashboard in case he slams on the brakes, and my stomach lurches as he ignores the Give Way sign at the top of a rise. Too quickly, we are on the other side of town.

'The local cemetery,' he says, jerking his head to the left.

'Thanks for that bit of comforting information, Dad.'

'Hang on. There are a few bends ahead.' We approach the first. He manipulates the gears like a rally driver but takes the badly banked curve way too fast. I inhale sharply.

'What's your problem?' he asks.

'There's no rush, Dad. The light's not too good,' I say, wondering what his night vision is like.

Further on he points to the right. 'That's the golf course.'

'You never played golf, did you?'

'No, it's a mug's game. But the clubhouse has a pretty good restaurant with some decent tucker.'

And a well-stocked bar, I'll bet.

After a straight stretch at the top of a ridge, he brakes and drags the wheel sharply to the left. 'Well, here we are,' he announces as we clunk rather too fast over a speed hump at the entrance. Mountain View Retirement Village, a sign announces.

The complex is quiet, with only a few lights dimmed by shutters, curtains, and vertical blinds. The units are enveloped in lush tropical plants, and there's a heady mix of perfumed blooms and recently turned soil. Could it have been the beauty of the tropical landscape that attracted him – a place of sugar cane, blood-red sunsets, and hovering mountain ranges?

I doubt it.

'What made you choose this place, Dad?' I ask.

His answer surprises me. 'The river … I'm thinking of getting a boat.'

At 78!

'What kind? A trailer boat?'

'Don't be bloody stupid. A decent-sized cruiser, something I can moor permanently on the river and sleep on overnight.'

Oh, of course. What a dill! He had spent much of his adult life in and around boats on Georges River and Botany Bay, and like Ratty in the Kenneth Grahame classic *The Wind in the Willows*, there was nothing that Dad thought 'half as much worth doing as simply messing about in boats'.

'You can go upriver from here for about 60 klicks,' he says, 'and there are plenty of safe nooks for mooring.'

'But you wouldn't go out through the Tweed Heads, would you?'

'Why not?' he asks.

'Well, not at your age, surely? And alone?'

'You never know *what* I might do.'

He's right about that.

Decades before, he would have relished the risk of crossing the dangerous Tweed Heads bar and heading out to sea, pitting himself against the breakers and swell. He was made in the mould of present-day round-the-world lone sailors, although he was a 'stink boat' man. He preferred to master nature with a motor than be at the mercy of the winds.

He lets me out of the car with more jiggling and tugging, waits for the garage roller door to close, and leads the way down a path winding through flowering hibiscus bushes, past a covered BBQ area and a half-sized bowling green.

'This is great, Dad,' I say, hoping he thinks it is, although I'm not sure about the bowling green. Not his style. But I *can* imagine him gathering with his neighbours for happy hour in the gazebo, or cooking a prime piece of rump steak on the gas BBQs with Tupperware bowls of potato and rice salad prepared by the women.

Or maybe not.

Dad's a bit of a contradiction, really; he's never had any problem socialising, but he likes to be in charge. And of course, Mum's not with him now.

'That's the lake,' he says, indicating a dark expanse across a strip of garden. 'Pretty full at the moment.'

'I'll go for a walk in the morning and do a bit of exploring,' I say as he fiddles with a bunch of keys.

He stands aside. 'There you go.' But in the dim light from a table lamp, I fail to see a can of insect spray placed just inside the front door. It rattles across the entrance tiles, the sound echoing in the still night.

'For the bugs,' he says and puts it back in place. He locks the door and secures the chain.

The unit smells of the stuffiness of a place rarely aired and of nose-tingling insect spray. And there's something else: the odour of loneliness. Or is that simply a misreading on my part of Dad's present situation?

'You're in here,' he says, depositing my bag in the master bedroom. 'I'm hitting the sack now, see you in the morning.'

'All right if I take a shower before I go to bed?'

'The towels are in there,' he says, pointing out the linen cupboard, and disappears into the toilet, where he'll wait for the intermittent flow of his piss.

*

I try imagining the conversation he would have had with the urologist when he was first diagnosed back in 1990.

'Well, give me the low-down, Doc?'

'Prostate cancer, I'm afraid, Greg. That's the bad news. But the good news is that it's localised. Hasn't spread beyond the prostate gland yet.'

'So what am I looking at then?'

'Well, because this is not an aggressive cancer like others, and because of your age and other medical conditions, I wouldn't recommend any radical treatment. If you live another ten years – maybe even more – it's unlikely you'll succumb to the disease. You're more likely to die of some other condition.'

'So what you're saying is that you're throwing me on the scrapheap because I'm in my seventies.'

'No, that's not what I'm saying, Greg. I'm saying that in your case, the cancer is unlikely to pose a threat. We adopt what is called a Watchful Waiting policy that involves a regular set of serum PSA measurements taken every six months or yearly, and regular examinations of the prostate.'

'So if I live into my early eighties, this cancer probably won't kill me.'

'I can't say *won't*, but it's highly unlikely. Many old men die *with* prostate cancer present, but not *of* it. In your case, high blood pressure is more of a problem.'

'Okay, so Watchful Waiting it is.'

'That's what I recommend at the moment.'

'But what about my peeing problem?'

'There's no blood in your urine, and you say there's no pain urinating, in which case I can give you some medication that will help.'

'Christ, I'll be rattling around like coins in an old tin with all the bloody pills you've pushed on me lately.'

'Then I suggest you help yourself with a few basic lifestyle changes, Greg. Take time to read through this pamphlet.'

Which, of course, he wouldn't have.

*

There's a tug on my heart at the sight of the double bed he's made up with worn pink sheets and yellow pillow slips – and a photo of Mum on the bedside table, the last one taken of her before she died. She's dressed in a lavender linen suit, and her fine white hair that started going grey in her twenties looks as if she's just come from the hairdressers, but osteoporosis has made her look very frail and far too old for someone only seventy-five when the picture was taken. She would have hated it.

I unpack my case and check out the wardrobe. It's full of Dad's suits and collared shirts and ties, but I suspect the last time he wore a suit was at Mum's funeral. The drawers in the bedside tables and bureau are all empty, except for one filled with incontinence pads. The linen cupboard is stacked with towels – mostly thin and worn – that came from the house he built in 1960, and also some striped flannelette sheets used by Mum in the Sydney winters, unlikely to be of much use in Murwillumbah. I choose a towel I remember: pink with maroon flowers.

In the bathroom, the shower curtain has a wide hem of mildew. There's a creamy white plastic chair in the alcove, but the shower recess shows no sign of recent use: the body grease collected in the tile grouting is pale, and there's no soap in the container, no face washer, and no shampoo, only a pair of stained underpants hanging stiffly from the hot-water tap.

I search for soap in the mirrored cupboard. There's none, just a rusted circle from a tin of something long since discarded, an electric shaver, a comb with a tooth missing, Rexona roll-on deodorant, a worn toothbrush, and a carefully rolled tube of Colgate toothpaste. When we were kids, he used to rant if anyone squeezed the toothpaste tube from the top rather than the bottom.

There's no soap in the vanity cupboard underneath the basin either, but behind eight rolls of toilet paper, I discover something that sets off a groan deep down in my gut: Mum's set of hot rollers and a few bobby pins.

Oh my God, did he miss her so much that he wanted to keep something personal of her near him: the rollers she used every day to make her thin hair presentable and the bobby pins used occasionally to keep a stray lock in place?

He was a man I never saw cry, a man who never said he couldn't go on, and yet these few ordinary objects belonging to Mum – who never made it Up North – show me more about him than if he had ever collapsed with grief.

I remove the chair and the undies and step into the shower recess, minus soap, allowing the heated water to ease the tension in my body and wash away the tears that I can no longer hold back. The shower chair, heated rollers, worn sheets and towels from long ago; the unused suits, once so proudly worn; the empty drawers, the incontinence pads, the photo taken just before Mum's death – it's all suddenly too much.

3

A Sleeping Bag and a Lladro Figurine

Something sharp digs into my shoulder; it's Mum lying beside me, framed in silver. I return her to the bedside table and then lie back and allow my senses to become more acute, taking in the slivers of light knifing through vertical blinds, the repeated chirrup of a bird, the flush of the toilet, and a running tap. Dad is up and at it already, whatever 'it' is. The front door opens, closes, and is double-locked.

I wait ten minutes or so and then roll out of bed and open the blinds. About 4 to 6 metres away is the lake. Two speckled ducks waddle from marsh grasses and reeds bordering a wooded island and propel themselves across the glassy surface. Close to the front door, a honeyeater hangs upside down feeding on the nectar of a shrub with pink tube-like flowers.

In the bathroom, there's a pair of recently washed underpants dripping in the shower recess and a damp towel, but still no evidence of his having taken a shower. Down the hall, on a single bed in the smallish second bedroom where he spent the night, there is a dark blue sleeping bag. It's one of those he and Mum used in their retirement camper van – the 'booze bus', we used to call it. These were the best sleeping bags on the market keeping them snug as they travelled the highways, country roads, and narrow rutted dirt tracks. Their camper van was always stocked with Scotch and white wine for the daily happy hour at the next campsite or caravan park.

He has already made his bed. The sleeping bag, with one corner folded back to reveal the tartan lining, is laid out neatly like a doona on a yellow chenille bed cover, a temporary arrangement for the duration of my stay.

The closed vertical blinds – backlit by the morning sun – give the room a soft buttery glow, but with a twist of the cord, shafts of light shimmering with dust motes highlight a talcum-powder-like coating on the furniture. Outside the room, there's a small sun-drenched garden and an empty clothesline.

In the kitchen, the stainless steel sink and taps are meticulously clean, almost in a pristine state, probably what you'd expect from a man who worked all his life with various types of steel. The cupboards are filled with neatly stacked tins of Ardmona fruit, SPC spaghetti and baked beans, and John West red salmon and asparagus. Dad always did buy in bulk. I'm not snooping, just looking for teabags; there'll be no loose tea, I know that.

Eventually, I find the teabags stored in a brown pottery canister, but I can't find a kettle or electric jug. He returns from wherever he's been to catch me on my hands and knees with my head in a cupboard under the sink. Shit!

'What the hell are you up to?'

'Looking for a kettle or jug to boil water … for a cuppa.'

'Use the microwave.'

'You can't make a decent cup of tea in the microwave, Dad.'

'My coffee's okay that way.'

'Well, I don't like my tea done like that.'

He shakes his head in exasperation and says, 'You'll find an electric jug somewhere in the back of that cupboard.' He hoists himself onto the kitchen bar stool and skims the front page of the morning paper.

'Dad,' I say, 'I feel bad sleeping in your bed. I would have been fine in the second bedroom.'

'Don't bloody worry about it. I don't sleep in the front room anymore.'

I wait to see if he'll elaborate; he doesn't. 'Wouldn't you be more comfortable in the double bed?'

He removes his glasses, and I wonder if I'm beginning to irritate him. 'Haze and I shared a bed for fifty-five years, and I kept waking up wondering why she wasn't there beside me. Then I'd remember. So I moved into the single bed. It's better that way.'

I say nothing and turn away, my eyes blurred. He won't appreciate me teary-eyed.

'I use a sleeping bag now. That way, I don't have to keep stripping and remaking the bed. Just wash and dry the bag and throw it back on.'

My eyes continue to sting, so I divert the conversation. 'Remember how tough you were on us when we were kids about making our beds properly?' I laugh. 'Spent hours showing us how to do the corners of the sheets. Like folding a package. Couldn't go out to play until we'd passed muster.'

'Gotta teach kids how to do things properly from the start,' he says and returns to his news headlines.

I take my mug of tea and head for the backyard to sit in the sun, but as I pass through the laundry, I see five pairs of shoes lined up neatly opposite the tubs, all covered with a furry white-green mould. He used to be fanatical about clean and polished shoes when we lived at home. 'You're not going to school with shoes like that. Get outside and polish them until you can see your face in them.' But now he seems selective in what he cleans.

Trousers soak in the laundry tub. 'Would you like me to rinse your pants and peg them on the line?' I call out. 'They'll be dry in no time.'

'Just leave them where they are. I'll put them in the dryer later.'

I shake my head and walk out to his lovely sunny backyard.

*

He's furnished his living room with a forest-green three-seater and two recliners; a round wooden country-style dining table and chairs; ceramic lamps with mushroom fabric shades; and a bookcase with only one shelf of books and scattered framed photos sent by various members of the family.

I picture him going into the one and only decent furniture store in Murwillumbah and, without too much deliberation, saying, 'I'll take those … and those … and those … and that and that.' Wouldn't have worried too much about colour and style. Probably took him no more than half an hour to furnish the unit.

But I notice, scattered about the room, a few things he's brought from Sydney: several long, low coffee or side tables – black metal with white laminated surfaces, tables he made himself in the seventies. And surprisingly, on one of them – totally out of place – is a delicate pink, blue, and white porcelain Lladro figurine. As far as I know, Dad has never really understood the emotional value of decorative objects.

'I see you kept Mum's Lladro.'

'What?'

'The seated ballerina.'

'Oh yeh, my girl liked that.'

'I'm glad you kept it,' I say, knowing he kept very little else.

The presence of Mum's rollers and the Lladro figurine in the Murwillumbah unit challenges my long-held view of Dad as lacking sentimentality.

I pick up the ballerina and carefully turn her upside down, noting the bluebell-flower logo on the base. I run my left hand over her satiny head, tutu, and legs. As I set her down again on the coffee table, I decide I will have her when the time comes. Something of Mum's, and something to remind me of a little-known side of my father.

4

Further Unexpected Surprises

One of Dad's great interests for years has been to check through the Sydney *Morning Herald* for machinery, motors, boats, or property, but now it's the *Daily Telegraph* with its crosswords. As part of his morning ritual, he winds his way uphill through the shimmering greens of palms and banana trees to the news agency at the top of the village. He chatters briefly and then ambles back home down one of the twisting paths.

Once inside, he fills a bowl with two Vita Brits and milk, places it in the microwave along with a cup of Nescafe, and waits for the beeps before he turns on the lamp over the kitchen bench. The blinds in his unit remain closed because the morning light worries his eyes. He settles on his wooden bar chair to read the news and then folds the crossword page into a square with the 'big one' face-up. With a stub of a pencil in his equally stubby fingers, a dictionary on one side, and a magnifying glass on the other, he begins.

'Can you get me the Macquarie thesaurus from my desk, love,' he asks.

In his office, separated from the lounge room by louvered folding doors, there's a bank of grey steel filing cabinets and a tidy desk with piles of bills, bank statements, and notices stapled together, an old mug filled with ballpoint pens, a small container of coloured paper clips, and his chequebook at the ready. But no thesaurus.

'It's not on your desk, Dad.'

'Try the bookshelves then.'

I run my index finger along the spines: a volume of Reader's Digest Condensed Books; four Alistair MacLean novels; several Wilbur Smith from the Courtney and Ballantyne series. Surprisingly, at the end of the row, along with the thesaurus, are two of my published books on ancient Greece and Rome.

My mind reels back ten years to the day when I took my hot-off-the-press book, *Ancient Greece: Using Evidence*, to show my parents. Mum was enthusiastic, of course. She was proud of everything I did and loved to brag to her friends at View Club about her children. Dad, on the other hand, had a thing about his kids – even as adults – getting swelled heads.

'Take a look at this, Greg,' Mum said and handed him the book with its cover of a Hellenistic onyx cameo of Alexander the Great and his mother, Olympias. But Dad's never been into history. Thirty years before, he had been less than impressed when I chose the humanities to study, declaring them 'useless, unproductive subjects'.

He sipped his Scotch and water, gave my first published book a quick once-over, and asked, 'How much money are you going to make out of this type of writing?'

'I've got no idea, Dad, probably not much.'

'Well, it's a bloody waste of effort if you're not going to have anything worthwhile to show for it. Why don't you put your energies into something that will make you a decent quid?'

'Dad, money isn't always the motivation.'

'Well, it should be.'

As I retrieve the thesaurus, my mind slips further back, as it has done often over the years, to 1955 when I first came to believe that no matter what I did, it would probably never be quite good enough for him. 'Pam, if you can get 98 per cent, you can get 100.' And I am overcome with a rush of hurt and a childish need to dump the thesaurus on the bench in front of him and say, 'Why couldn't you just once have given me some bloody praise?'

Instead, I say, 'I'm surprised to see two of my books on the shelf.'

'Yes, just boxed up what was in the Sydney flat when your mother died.'

*

'I think I'll take a walk around the village,' I say. 'Want to come?'

'No, I'm okay here with my crossword.'

Just outside the front door, beside a cobweb-covered air conditioner, is an old chair, its metal corroded and its faded green vinyl covered in bird shit. Why the hell would a man with so much money have a chair like that on the front patio of an expensive unit? Why would he have kept it all these years and brought it Up North with him? I can understand the rollers, the Lladro, and to a certain extent, the metal and laminated coffee tables, but not the bomb of a car he bought, and not this old metal fold-up chair.

Maybe he planned to tinker with the car. After all, he had spent a lifetime tinkering with motors. But what was his attachment to the old chair? Could it have been the first one he ever made, in the days when he made everything?

I cross the paved path to the lake, its water dark and still except for a ripple. From somewhere among the tangle of vines and grasses on the artificial island comes a sharp guttural crowing. Then I hear footsteps. A tall woman strides towards me. I smile and say good morning, but she seems perturbed to see a stranger on the path and lowers her head.

'And a nice day to you too,' I say softly after she passes.

I make my way past grevilleas and frangipani into a stand of stringent-smelling eucalypts that edge the lake. There's the odour of rotting vegetation, flashes of crimson rosellas in the trees above, and the cacophony of cheeky lorikeets squabbling over the nectar of a bottlebrush. Further along, up towards the Rainforest Units – as opposed to the Lakeside Units – I hear a raking sound in the undergrowth. It's a brush turkey scrounging around in the leaf litter for seeds, fallen fruit, and insects.

Two more women amble round the bend in the path: one wearing a synthetic maroon tracksuit and joggers and the other in a floral skirt, cotton twin set, and sturdy walking shoes. I step aside, smile, and try another 'good morning'. This time there's a response.

'Are you new here?' Tracksuit asks, and I wonder if I really look that old.

'Visiting my father for a few days. From Sydney.'

'So which unit does he live in?'

'Back down there by the bottom of the lake,' I say. 'Ground floor.'

They look at each other and smirk. 'You mean Greg?' Floral Skirt asks.

I nod.

'We've tried getting him up to the village centre to join in the activities,' says Tracksuit, 'but he's not interested.'

'Well, good luck with that,' I say, wondering about the smirk between them. 'Enjoy your walk.'

Further on, a motorised buggy sporting a limp red flag passes me at a snail's pace with a grind and a whir.

Dad is not in his unit when I return. I discover him sunning himself on an outdoor setting adjacent to the bowling green, his glasses and keys lying on the table, his shirt off, his eyes closed against the glare. Except for his gut, his body is not too bad for an old bloke of close to seventy-nine: broad chest and the outline of muscles – once as hard as steel – still discernible under the slack skin of his upper arms. I wonder if a bare-chested Dad was what the smirk between Tracksuit and Floral Skirt was about. He always was – and still is apparently – a man unhampered by self-consciousness.

I join him on the bench, and he opens his eyes. 'Well, how was it?'

'Beautiful. I bumped into a few of your fellow residents along the path.'

'Yes, the old ducks walk around the lake on their morning constitutionals.'

'What about you?'

'Occasionally.'

'I noticed a village bus parked outside the administration centre. Does it ferry residents to and from town?'

'A few times a day.'

'Do you ever use it?'

He gives one of his *are you a dill* looks. 'Wouldn't be caught dead in it,' he says and then changes the subject. 'Did you see the eels in the lake?'

'Well, I saw a ripple.'

'Could have been a water snake.' He stares at the lake as if looking for something. 'See over there,' he says and points to a grey and white tail visible above the water. 'A moorhen.' The bird in question surfaces: dark grey-black with a red facial shield and a yellow-tipped bill. 'I think there's a breeding group. I've counted at least five of them. If you climb down that embankment there, you might be able to see their nests among the reeds.'

'Don't tell me you've been climbing down that muddy slope?' I ask.

He ignores me. Whether it's deliberate or due to his poor hearing, I can't say. 'There are a few different species of ducks too,' he continues. 'And brush turkeys in the bush along the path.' Once again, he's completely surprised me. Although he's always been an outdoors-type of bloke, I've never thought of him before as being particularly interested in natural habitats. And yet, here he is telling me about the varied water life outside his unit. Is it possible that I never really knew him very well, or is it that as we get older and spend more time alone we see the beauty in things around us that we once overlooked?

The motorised-buggy woman is on her second round of the lake, and I ask if there are many men in the village. 'Yes, but they're all a bunch of bloody old codgers,' he says.

'Really?' I laugh.

We slip into silence. He appears to be focussed on the lake, and I wonder if this is the closest he ever gets to meditation. Two more women appear, one with a clicking cane. Dad stretches his shoulders back, squints, and puts on his glasses, the sun glinting on the metal frames.

'Wondered where you girls were this morning.'

They smile. 'A beautiful day,' says Cane.

'How are you today, Greg?' asks the other, rather elegant one with soft hair like Mum's.

'Entertaining my daughter. Taking her off to lunch later.'

'Enjoy it,' says Cane.

'Have a nice day,' adds the Mum lookalike, and they keep walking.

I doubt if Dad knows their names, and I suspect he has never had a meaningful conversation with any of the women who pass his unit every day. But perhaps I'm wrong. After all, he has already started taking on a different shape in my mind, and I've been here less than a day.

5

A Country Pub and Salvador Dali

It's eleven thirty, and he's ready and waiting to go to lunch.

'Bit early, isn't it?' I ask.

'Like to be there by noon,' he says.

'So where are we going then?'

'The Australian Tavern. Young Sue's on today.'

'And *she* is?'

'The waitress.' He doesn't elaborate, and I wonder if he fancies her.

The drive to town is uncomfortable. He screeches around the bends near the cemetery, and as I plead with him to slow down, he laughs and calls me a wuss. I refrain from commenting as he scrunches into the narrow space of the supermarket car park, but on the way to the tavern, I offer to drive home so that he can enjoy a few drinks.

'What are you suggesting?' His mouth is grim.

'Nothing really,' I lie.

He shakes his head. 'No need.'

Right!

As we round the corner to the pub, the acrid smell of cigarette smoke wafts in our faces. Its source is an unkempt old man leaning against a wall to one side of the entrance. A dog lead dangles from his yellow-stained right hand – no sign of a dog though – and a limp roll-your-own cigarette hangs from chapped lips. He takes a last drag and flicks the butt, still glowing, onto the pavement.

'Filthy, stinking habit,' says Dad, making no effort to hide his disgust or lower his voice.

'You used to smoke, if I remember correctly,' I say.

'Only on social occasions, never addicted. Could stop any time I wanted.'

The smoker doubles over racked with a fit of coughing. Dad digs a five-dollar note from his trouser pocket and thrusts it at him. 'Stop smoking those bloody cancer sticks, mate.'

The old bloke nods, stuffs the note in his shirt pocket, and then whistles. A blue heeler shambles from a narrow recess with something in his mouth and waits patiently while his owner attaches the lead to his collar.

'That's so sad,' I say, watching them disappear around the corner.

'Don't waste your bloody sympathy.'

Excuse me, who just gave the man five dollars?

In the public bar, there's a scattering of men, some talking, some saying nothing, just flushed faces glued to the TV watching a cricket test replay. One with an alcoholic glaze stares at the froth oozing down the side of his schooner and belches. In a corner, two tradies in grey shorts and shirts attack their beef pies, while at the pool table, a girl – late adolescence, wearing tight slashed jeans, her face hidden by stringy blonde hair – balances the cue and then shoots. 'Fuck it,' she yells as she misses the pocket. Her two companions bray like donkeys, and one spills his beer on the carpet as he gives the girl a light punch on the upper arm.

'Cop the jeans on that one, torn to pieces.'

'I think that's probably the latest fashion, Dad.'

'That's not fashionable. Your mother was fashionable. And anyway, they should be at work.'

'Maybe it's their lunch break.'

'No, not them, they're dole bludgers. Let them get off their lazy backsides and find work. It shouldn't be that hard. And if they can't get a job, they shouldn't be wasting their bloody money on beers.'

There's no point in arguing.

Once in the dining room, his antenna is up, searching out Sue – who appears from the kitchen, her arms laden with plates. 'Be with you in a minute, Greg,' she calls. 'Your usual table's available.'

He leads me to it, pulls out my chair, waits for me to settle, and then takes his place facing the kitchen, coffee machine, and cash register. I note his appreciative gaze and half smile as he follows Sue around the room and in and out of the kitchen and wonder if a bit of flirting adds a little brightness to his days. Then she's at his side. Much younger than I'd expected, no more than twenty-five I'd guess. He introduces me.

'What about wine, Greg? Riesling?'

'That okay, darl?'

'Fine, Dad.'

'Had a chance to check the menu yet?' she asks. 'Or are you going to stick with the prawns, Greg?' We decide: garlic prawns, and a dessert of bread and butter pudding for him, a pasta for me.

He watches her disappear into the kitchen. 'Nice small bum,' he says. 'Not like most of the women up here with their huge backsides.'

And then, as if on cue and to illustrate his point, two obese women – possibly mother and daughter – enter the restaurant and make their way to a table on the opposite side of the room. 'Look, there go a couple of monsters,' he points out rather too loudly. 'Murbah-big-bums,' he says and laughs. 'Never seen so many in one place in all my life. Not like your mother; she had the perfect derrière.'

Can we please let it go? I try directing the conversation onto something interesting, something other than Mum's perfect bum and the monsters on the other side of the room. But my attempts produce nothing but mechanical responses. Nascent words, phrases, and sentences dry up like autumn leaves, and a silence stretches between us. I never did experience the rhythm of easy, compatible talk with him.

Rather too quickly, we consume the bottle of Riesling. He upends it in the ice bucket, waves to Sue, and orders another. She uncorks the bottle, and as he turns towards her, I examine his unlined face. It's so unfair that men don't seem to wrinkle as much as women. On the other hand, he has a network of fine red and purple spider veins in his nose, which now seem to have taken on a Riesling glow.

Thankfully, our meal arrives, relieving me of trying to keep the conversation going. Since he's not going to let me drive home, I drink as much as I can of the second bottle.

As soon as he's finished his dessert, he calls for the bill. Oh yes, by all means, let's not linger over a leisurely lunch.

He withdraws an American Express platinum card, adds a more than reasonable tip to the bill, signs with a flourish, and snaps the black folder closed. He digs into his fob pocket for a folded twenty-dollar bill.

'This is for you, love,' he says to Sue, slipping the note into her hand.

She gives him a cheeky smile and pats him on the shoulder. 'Thanks, Greg.' He watches her go, his smile fading.

'Tomorrow, we'll go to the Imperial,' he says, 'the pink pub in the main street. Helen, who manages the bistro, is real nice.'

'I thought you were keen on Sue.'

'She's got two days off.'

God, he even knows her roster!

'Well, what now?' I say.

'What do you mean?'

'What are we going to do now?'

'Go home, of course.'

'But it's not even one thirty.'

'Well, *I'm* going home; you please yourself. You can stay here if you want. Catch a cab back.'

I walk with him to the car and wave him off with mixed feelings: a sense of relief that I don't have to struggle to make conversation for a few hours, and anxiety, knowing now of his daily routine of quaffing a bottle or two of white wine with lunch. I wait until he backs out of the narrow space and heads for the car park exit.

Dad was right. There certainly seem to be a lot of big bums wobbling, swaying, and bouncing up and down the main shopping strip, along with pregnant women and mothers with babies in strollers: a fertile environment in more ways than one.

The street is lined with the usual country-style pubs and cluttered, old-fashioned stores, plus shops selling crystals, incense, and psychic readings as well as natural therapies. There are plenty of coffee shops and places to eat – some vegetarian, run by hippy types.

In an arcade, I discover a bizarre café decorated with memorabilia of the Spanish painter Salvador Dali. No fine art collectibles, but plenty of melting clocks, small statuettes of Don Quixote and matadors, photos of the artist himself and ceramic heads, a print of his 'Butterflies', reproductions of his hideous Divine Comedy series, and surrealist mugs and postcards. Judging by the adverts posted on the wall, it appears to be a gathering place for local writers and artists.

I think about ringing Dad to check that he got back okay, but I won't. I can imagine his response: 'What the hell is wrong with you? You think I'm a little kid?'

I settle down with a pot of English breakfast tea, jot in my journal, and ponder on why I made the long train trek Up North. Was it for his benefit or mine? Did I naively think that we might be able to establish a real companionable relationship now that we were both older, now that he no longer had Mum? Was I perhaps hoping to gain some kudos by appearing to be a good and caring daughter? Or was I simply checking that he was okay in order to reassure the family?

Probably all of the above.

6

Thoughts in a Tweed Valley Cemetery

I decide against taking a taxi; it's a good day for walking, and I have an impulse – before tackling the bendy incline – to make a detour through the cemetery with its stunning views over the Tweed Valley.

There's a warm calm among the pitted and cracked headstones with their lichen-filled inscriptions speaking of so many tragedies and lives cut short. I sit for a while between the resting place of a twenty-six-year-old male killed by a falling tree during a storm and a 5-year-old girl who drowned in the Tweed River. I close my eyes. A childhood memory plays like an old film on the back of my eyelids.

Dad had just manoeuvred the curves along the spooky mangrove-lined Minnamurra River on the NSW south coast. When he reached Bombo, with its darkly ominous volcanic cliffs, he pulled over and parked opposite the cemetery. My stomach clenched, and I slid down behind the driver's seat, hunched over, eyes tightly shut. He returned from checking on the flapping tarpaulin covering the trailer packed with camping gear and Christmas presents.

'Pam, you're not bunging on that act again, are you? How many times do I have to tell you there's nothing bad in that graveyard. No ghosts, no monsters.' Even so, my heart beat rapidly. 'Come on. Get out of the car. Here, hold my hand, and I'll prove it once and for all. Nothing's going to happen to you. It's just your imagination.'

Mum told him to leave me be and to just get going, but he dragged me out of the car and across the road. 'Don't be stupid, open your eyes,' he said. I inhaled and exhaled in quick gasps as his firm hand guided me among the headstones. He kept his voice soft, talking about what we were going to do on holidays: how he'd teach me to skim stones across the lagoon and fish with bread for poddy mullet from the bridge; how we'd climb the headland, chase crabs in the rock pools, and dress up in kelp skirts; and about Christmas morning. On and on he went until I began to breathe more slowly. Then he eased himself onto a dirty white stone slab and lowered me down beside him. The sun was warm, a bird warbled nearby, and he began to sing too, although I don't remember what he sang that day. We remained there for a while until Mum called out, 'Come on, gotta get going.'

'See, nothing to be scared of,' he said. And I don't think I ever bunged on that act again.

Triggered by the nearby headstone of the drowned 5-year-old, the past continues to slide into the present: the lagoon at Werri Beach on the South Coast, and a child absorbed in her sandcastle with its tunnels, turrets, and moat.

I was patting, smoothing, and shovelling with my plastic bucket and spade when I felt his hand on my arm. 'Come on, time to swim.'

I looked to Mum for support, but she simply indicated for me to go with him and rolled over on her bright red towel.

With his hand supporting my belly, he led me into deep water and let go. 'Swim,' he said, and I was on my own. I panicked, but he ignored the desperate thrashings, just stood and watched as I tried to touch the sandy bottom with my pointed toes. But it was not there, and I went under. He dragged me up. I was spluttering for precious air.

'Daddy ... Daddy ...'

'Swim,' he said sharply.

And I did, instinctively dog-paddling all the way back to shore. 'See, you *can* do it,' he said as he lifted me out.

His first lesson in survival accomplished.

*

I continue to sit among the dead, and my mind turns to Mum. Her ashes are in a rose garden under a bronze plaque in Woronora Cemetery in Sydney's south. The adjacent spot is waiting for Dad.

It's was a bright blue Easter Tuesday, not quite two years ago, when we followed her coffin into South Chapel and took our places in the pews on the right. Dad didn't shed a tear, but my voice wavered as I gave the eulogy, finishing with: 'Throughout her life, Mum was an elegant, diplomatic, and dignified woman ... always the love of Dad's life. Of all her attributes, the one for which she was most admired was her ability to subtly and lovingly castigate and control the man who was beside her for well over half a century …'

He squeezed my arm when I returned to my seat, and I wondered just how strong he was. Several days before the funeral – perhaps still in shock – he had dressed in his best suit and joined in the celebration of his grandson's wedding, and then returned home alone to deal with his grief. I often wondered how long it was before he became fully aware of his devastating loss. What impact would a sudden death at home in a shared bed have?

I think now about him with his prostate cancer, his high blood pressure, glaucoma; his consumption of a bottle of wine with lunch; and his bloody over-confidence as he swings his small rusty bomb round the bends and past the cemetery twice a day. There's a heavy despairing feeling in my solar plexus.

I can't stand the thought of him being up here on his own, with no one to care about him. He could die in that unit by the lake: trip on the way to the toilet in the dark, slip in the shower (on the rare occasions he takes one), have a stroke watching TV, and no one would know. The old women would continue to pass by on their daily walks, maybe casually wondering why they hadn't seen him but not thinking too much about it.

And what about us Down South? Would we be overly worried if he didn't answer his phone for a few days? Probably gone up to his unit on the Gold Coast, we'd think, consulting with Dawn the real estate 'girl', contemplating another property purchase. When would we start to consider checking up on him? Of course, we'd probably hear if he failed to take a bend near the cemetery.

A gentle spring breeze disturbs the branches as I begin the winding uphill climb. But an odd sensation of guilt shadows me.

It's almost quarter past five by the time I reach the village entrance; I'd underestimated the difficulty of the climb. The unit is locked up and the blinds are pulled, but there's a flickering bluish light and spikes of laughter. The television is on. I knock several times, but he doesn't hear. I bang on the windows; there's no response. I call out and then flop in the fold-up chair with its bird shit, place my bag on the cobwebbed air conditioner, and consider what to do if I can't get him to answer the door. There's always the motel on the edge of town, I guess. I give the door one more pounding and shout at the top of my voice.

There's a jangling of keys, a clang of metal on metal, and the door opens. He's in his pyjamas. 'No need to break the bloody door down,' he says. 'Just remember in the future, I always lock up at five.'

'Right, total lockdown at five. I'll try to remember.'

7

Tracksuit and Tucker Time at Tumbulgum

I return to Sydney with a permanent sense of unease and a vague ache in my heart – but absorbed, as we are, in our families and everyday challenges, my siblings and I know little of what is happening to Dad Up North.

Six months pass. This time, I fly to Coolangatta, hire a car, drive south to Murwillumbah, and book into a motel where there is no five o'clock lockout. When I ring to tell him I've arrived, he says, 'It's a bit late, isn't it?'

'Well, I'm not popping in right *now*, Dad,' I say, wondering what it would be like to be really welcomed by one's parent. 'I'll catch up with you in the morning.'

I pour myself a glass of Chardonnay and go out to the balcony. The air is clammy; thunder reverberates in the foothills and lightning veins thread through obese clouds. Raindrops as big as fifty-cent coins begin to fall, creating patterns like some impressionist painting on the dry pavement. Then the rain starts in earnest, a curtain lowered over the mountainous backdrop of Mount Warning where the dawn sun first touches eastern Australia. It buckets down, drumming hard on the roof of the motel and ricocheting off the bonnets of the cars parked below, hissing as it hits the heated bitumen of the road. Within minutes, the motel's guttering is unable to cope, and the overflow splashes onto the balcony. But I remain where I am, enjoying its cooling effect and the spectacular flickering light show over the McPherson and Tweed Ranges.

By the time I'm onto my second glass of wine, the storm has passed. The purple sky turns to late afternoon flame, and the air is filled with the fecund smell of earth. A cicada chorus starts up again, drilling the air. Their singing is particularly loud this summer, the motel manager told me when I arrived. As the afternoon folds into night, crickets and frogs create a racket from somewhere in the backyard of an old Queenslander opposite, competing with a television in one of the motel rooms along the way.

It rains again during the night, and when I drive to the village, I find Dad in the garage squelching around in a pair of galoshes swishing out the excess water with a stiff broom, worrying about the wheels of his car. It's a different car. Not new, but different, slightly more modern. When I comment, he says, 'The other one had a few dings, and this one's got a better gearbox.'

All the same, I'll insist on being the driver this time, I think as I park the white automatic Ford hire car in the visitors' space.

He locks the garage, and we wind our way past the lake – which, after the recent downpour, is a muddy colour.

'Hi, Greg.' It's his upstairs neighbour, a man considerably younger than Dad dressed in bowling gear – definitely not an old codger. His wife, also dressed in whites and carrying a watering can, emerges from among the abundance of colour that explodes from all parts of their veranda. Hugh and Jean engage Dad in a few minutes of small talk regarding an interclub competition with a bowling team from Southport.

'They seem nice,' I say when we are inside the unit.

'They're okay. Don't have much to do with them really. Obsessed with bloody bowls.'

And the pain in my heart is there again.

'I've got a few things to do in the office before lunch, love,' he says. 'Make yourself a cuppa.'

The electric jug has been returned to its hiding place deep in the recesses of the saucepan cupboard, so I follow Dad's example: heat a mug of water in the microwave, dangle a teabag in the hot water, and perch on the kitchen stool. The yellowing pad beside the phone is filled with Dad's notes to himself in his distinctive hand. I see a number of grocery items – including custard, milk, and Arrowroot biscuits – and a list of people and phone numbers, including his bank manager, a name I recognise as his Murwillumbah solicitor, and a Dr Hunter.

The phone, which I never heard ring once on my last visit, breaks the silence. Two rings only.

'That'll be Eileen,' he calls out. 'She'll be on her way down for a cuppa.'

'Oh … so you've found yourself a girlfriend?'

'I wouldn't say *that*.'

It's not five minutes before there's a shuffle outside the front door followed by a knock. The woman standing at the door seems vaguely familiar. 'You here already?' she says. Shit! It's Tracksuit, the dumpy, nosey smirker I met on the path on my last visit.

Eileen-Tracksuit is everything Mum wasn't, someone Dad would have once described as 'last card in the pack'. I wonder why, if he was so keen for a friend, he didn't choose the elegant one with Mum's hair, or friendly Cane. Even Floral Skirt would have been a better choice. There must be any number of suitable women in the village. But perhaps they have 'old codger' husbands. Or maybe they're happy to be finally without a man. Of course, they might not fancy him.

'So, where're we going for lunch?' Eileen asks.

'Well, I'm driving,' I say before Dad can answer.

'Okay, the Tumby Pub then,' she decides.

'It's out of town,' Dad explains, 'on the Tweed at Tumbulgum.'

With that apparently decided, Eileen marches into the kitchen. 'Coffee?'

'Nothing for me, thanks,' I say.

She heats up two coffees in the microwave and puts three biscuits on a plate. 'Don't forget to make your doctor's appointment, Greg,' she says as she takes two of the biscuits and her mug and disappears into the tiny backyard.

'She'll be having a fag,' he says. 'Can't stand it. Close the bloody door,' he yells.

Shit, they're just like an old married couple. I wonder what has happened since I was here last.

'What did she mean about a doctor's appointment, Dad?'

'I just need to pick up a referral.'

'For what?'

'To see a specialist in Southport.'

'What kind of a specialist?'

'About the thing in my gut.' I wait. 'A small bulge,' he adds.

'A hernia?'

'No, something to do with the weakening of the blood-vessel wall.'

'Is it an aneurism?'

'It's not a major problem. It's only small.'

Not a major problem? 'If it's an aneurism, Dad, and you don't have it seen to, it could rupture.'

He's getting irritable. 'Yeh, yeh.'

'Dad, it could haemorrhage if it ruptures, and …'

'Yes, and I'll be dead. Okay. Just forget it. I'll have it seen to.'

*

I'm already fed up with Eileen's directions from the backseat as we leave Murwillumbah and head north. Just a short way along the Tweed Valley Highway, she yells, 'Turn here.' I swing the wheel.

'Watch it,' says Dad.

'Well, you could have given me a bit of advance warning.'

After another turn, we wind along the river through fields of sugar cane into a picturesque village with heritage shopfronts. 'Park there,' Dad instructs, pointing to a spot under the trees of a riverside picnic area adjacent to a public wharf. A boat from Tweed Heads, full of noisy day-trippers, is attempting to manoeuvre into position. 'He's not going to make it doing it that way,' Dad says, probably wishing he could take charge and show off his own boating skills.

Eileen has already crossed the street and is waiting at the entrance to the tavern, but Dad remains staring at the river, watching a boat skimming across the glassy surface pulling two skiers. I wonder if he's reminiscing about his pre-cruiser days when he hurtled around Georges River in *White Night*, his sleek aluminium powerboat.

He never did motor the Tweed River on his own. The river was really only suitable for boats 4 to 5 metres in length, and most were trailer boats. Also, to renew his NSW boat owner's licence, he would have had to take a practical course. Maybe he decided it was all too much of a hassle to be bothered with, but I can imagine how he felt when his dream of having a boat evaporated.

'Look at that shag!' he says, pointing to a black-faced cormorant perched on a dead branch that has fallen into the shallows, its long neck and pointed bill stretched horizontal to the water.

'Come on, Greg,' Eileen shouts from across the road. 'It's tucker time.'

Picnickers look up. He doesn't answer. He's still watching the shag watching the water.

'Tucker time,' she repeats, louder this time, her call mimicked by the harsh caw of a crow in a nearby tree.

'Eileen's hungry,' I say.

'She's always bloody hungry. Stuffs it down as if it's her last meal.'

'I suppose going to lunch with you saves her having to cook dinner.'

'Don't know; don't care. None of my business what she does most of the time.'

We cross the road, but Eileen has disappeared. She's taken up a position at a table near the window, and when we sit down, she immediately gives Dad her order. No manners whatever. 'Wait for Pam to look at the blackboard menu, Eileen.' He gives her a look I remember from my childhood. 'Want a pre-lunch drink, darl?' he says to me.

'Yes, but let me get it.'

'Greg'll pay,' Eileen pipes in.

'No he won't, Eileen. It's my shout.'

'Tooheys Draught, love. Lemon squash for her.'

'Oh, so you don't drink alcohol, Eileen?'

'I don't like boozers. Greg drinks too much.'

'She's referring to Fiji,' he says.

Don't tell me he took her to Fiji, the place he and Mum enjoyed so much.

'You were drunk all the time in Fidgee. It was a terrible holiday.'

I've had enough of this. 'Listen, Eileen, I'm up here to visit Dad, not you. If you don't approve of his ways, then don't accept his generosity.' I push back my chair and disappear to the bar.

Of course, Dad would never admit he'd had a drinking problem in the past, nor to being an argumentative rather than a happy, silly drunk. I'm not fond of myself either when I've had a few: rather too vehement in my opinions. But Dad seems to have cut back on the grog lately. There are no supplies in the unit, so I guess he only drinks at lunch.

While I wait for the barman, I check out the bistro food list. Obviously, Eileen and Dad know what they're having, and when I return, she's fidgety.

'Better feed Eileen,' I say to him.

'We'll have our drinks first,' he says, 'and then I'll order wine with lunch.'

'Give me the money, Greg, and I'll go and order,' Eileen says impatiently.

'Christ, woman! If you're that ravenous, go and place the orders, and get a bottle of Riesling for Pam and me while you're at it.' He hands her a hundred-dollar note.

I watch her low-slung bum sway all the way to the bistro counter. Not a Murbah-bum, but still too large for her height, definitely not a Mum or Sue backside, not an elegant woman in any way whatever.

'The people in the village don't like her much,' he says. 'She's quite bossy.'

You reckon? 'I don't mean to be rude, Dad, but it's a bit disappointing to see you with someone like her. There must be any number of women – something like Mum – in the village you could spend your time with.'

'I don't want anyone like your mother.'

I'm speechless.

'Don't look at me like that. No one could ever replace Haze. I don't even want someone who comes close. Eileen is the extreme opposite of your mother, a tough little nut I can take or leave.'

'Well, why bother at all?'

'Just used to having someone to take to lunch, that's all.'

And on expensive holidays. 'So you're lonely?'

'No, it's just a habit.'

'Lunch is one thing, Dad, but did you have to take her to Fiji?'

'She'd never had a holiday before,' he says. 'Had a hard life. But I must admit, it *was* a big mistake.'

Well that's a first. Admitting a mistake.

I catch a fleeting look, a reflection perhaps of a tender memory: Mum and him sitting in the late tropical sun at the Fijian's Bilo Bar, glasses of Scotch in their hands, watching a vermilion sun set over the coral-fringed lagoon and entertaining Albert the local bartender. No one cared if they were slightly tiddly; no one criticized their wobbly return to their room, arm in arm.

Eileen returns with the bistro buzzer and starts going on about some village issue: who is doing this and that, who said what, and the slack general manager who hasn't done something despite her constant complaints. Dad's not interested, but I listen and make the occasional comment. At least her chatter fills what would otherwise be extended silences if I were alone with him.

But he's had enough and changes the subject. 'You know this pub's been licensed since 1887,' he says to me. 'Did you get a look at all those photos on the wall over there?'

'Not yet, but I will.'

'Take a gander at the painting of the Tumbulgum Groper,' he adds. "It's only half the size of the real thing caught by a local fisherman 160 years ago. Weighed 800 pounds. Can you imagine that?'

'Do you think it might be just a pub tale?'

'Well, go and check the blurb written on the board.'

'Right,' I say, thankful for the opportunity to escape.

When I return to the table, I hear Eileen saying something about Dad's unit in the Iluka building on the Gold Coast.

'So you've been to the Iluka, Eileen?' I ask.

'Of course,' she answers proprietarily.

How could he? Now I'm really pissed off with him. Fiji *and* the Iluka.

8

A Cunning Old Bugger

His on-off relationship with Eileen is a source of endless gossip in the village, apparently, and I will admit that at times, as a family, we fear she might be after his money. Eventually, I give up caring about how different she is from Mum. It's Dad's life, and I am relieved that my solitary, irascible father has someone to go to lunch with, someone who is company for him when he decides he needs it, someone who reminds him of his doctor's appointments, buys him the occasional shirt, and rings us if she is worried about him. In many ways, it takes a load off my mind.

*

It's eight forty-five in the morning, and his phone has rung out twice already. I wait another fifteen minutes and try again, but still no answer, and I'm rather concerned. It's over an hour since he would have gone to collect the morning paper. I dial again, and this time he answers after four rings.

'Gregory Patrick Carlson, to whom am I speaking?'

'Hi, Dad, it's me.'

'Which *me* is that?'

'It's Pam. What have you been up to lately?'

'Waging war against the bloody spiders.'

Not exactly what I meant, although a killing rampage is one of his daily tasks, his weapon of choice a red can of Mortein Fast Knockdown insect spray. Scores of cans are stacked in the laundry cupboard – well, not scores exactly, but a lot – and a can is placed for convenience in each room. Really adds something to the décor, I must say.

'How have you been since we spoke last?'

'What's your problem?' he snaps.

'Just wondering how you are, Dad.'

'I'm okay, of course.'

There are no questions about what *I'm* up to, no stream of chatter about family news, nothing deep and meaningful. I struggle to think up questions to keep the conversation going: Does he need me to do anything for him? No, he is quite capable of looking after himself. Is he lonely? No, of course not. Has he been up to the Gold Coast recently? Yes, a few weeks ago. Is he buying more property? Could be. And so on.

'I'll be down on Tuesday,' he says. 'Have to go and see the quack in Macquarie Street about my eyes.'

'What time's your flight?'

'Just a sec,' he says. I hear the rustle of paper. He's probably got the details written in pencil on the old pad beside the phone. 'Leave Coolangatta at 10.45.'

'Okay, I'll meet you at the airport.'

'No need.'

'Well, catch a cab to the flat then and I'll come with you to the doctors. We can have some lunch.'

'See you later,' he says and hangs up.

*

I inhale the city's toxic fumes as I lean over the grimy railing of my unit in the heart of the city waiting for Dad to arrive from the airport. It's not really my unit; it belongs to him. When he decided to take off Up North after Mum's death, he offered it to my husband and me. Didn't offer it for free, of course; that wasn't his way.

In the stiff August breeze, delinquent sheets of newspaper catch at the legs of unsuspecting pedestrians twenty floors below, and a plastic bag floats phantom-like past the sixth floor. I watch the traffic hoping to see a cab pull up in front. The monorail rattles past the second floor and the roar of a motorbike echoes among the city canyons, but there are no cabs slowing down outside the Berkeley, and no sign of my 80-year-old father.

I focus on a spider descending on its web in a sheltered corner of the balcony and listen to the drifting wail of a Scottish piper performing outside Meyers Department Store. And like I once did as a mother, waiting for my teens to arrive home at some ungodly hour of the morning, I count cars. In those days, it was headlights moving down the St Ives hill; now it's occupied cabs. I give myself a target of ten. The seventh cab slows and pulls into the curb, and I exhale with relief. But it doesn't stop; instead, it veers across into the second lane to screeching brakes and abuse, and then it accelerates down Market Street. I count another ten and then go inside, closing the glass doors against the wind gusts.

Could he have confused the date? Missed the plane perhaps? Or decided 'bugger it' and gone to lunch somewhere in Murwillumbah to flirt with the waitresses?

As a distraction, I pick up the *Herald* from the coffee table and scan the news. John Howard, the prime minister, has been creating a controversy by avoiding the use of the word *sorry* for the past injustices suffered by indigenous Australians. He maintains that 'Australians of this generation should not be required to accept guilt and blame for past actions and policies.' Dad approves of Howard's attitude. He's never said sorry for anything he did as far as I can remember. 'Bloody waste of effort feeling guilty,' he'd say.

Needing to take some action, I haul down the heavy Yellow Pages directory from the cupboard above the oven and look up Macquarie Street ophthalmologists. I don't know which eye specialist he attends for his glaucoma, but I take a stab. No luck with the first two calls, but on the third, the receptionist says, 'Yes, Mr Carlson has been and gone. He came to the surgery early and demanded to be fitted in. Caused quite a fuss.'

Of course he did. He never could wait patiently for his turn, never stood in a queue, wasn't one for other people's timetables and rules. If he wasn't attended to immediately, he'd try charm first and then bluster. Sometimes he just left.

So where is he now?

It's possible he's having lunch alone at one of his old Sydney haunts, so I put on my coat, wrap a scarf around my neck, and take the lift to reception. My teenage sons used to call me a sniffing bloodhound, and I wonder how Dad will react if I happen to find him enjoying his lunch alone. But I won't be put off.

He's not at the Marketplace in the Hilton, and nobody at the Chan family's Fortune Village restaurant in the Bowler's Club has seen him. They all remember him, of course, despite his two-year absence – after all, he was a big tipper in his Sydney days – but they haven't seen him today. They want to stop and talk, relate funny anecdotes about him and the Princess, but I'm not in the mood, and I've heard them all before.

By four thirty, when I haven't heard a word from him, I ring his Murwillumbah number. Down the line comes: 'Gregory Patrick Carlson, to whom am I speaking?'

'Dad, it's me. What happened to you today?'

'Caught an earlier plane down, saw the quack, hailed a cab to the airport, and jumped on the next plane home,' he replies, self-satisfaction in his voice. Bastard. I should have known. That's been his modus operandi for years – disappearing without telling anyone.

He's been averse to coming Down South since he moved Up North, although he did make it down for his eightieth birthday and – under sufferance – attended a Christmas celebration and his first great-grandchild's naming day in the country town of Braidwood. As long as I can remember, he's always been a reluctant guest in other people's homes, even family. When he deigned to visit, it was always as if he were just passing through. He loathes people organizing him – and although I know it wasn't the case, one could be forgiven for thinking he deliberately sabotaged many of the events masterminded by others. I think he would prefer us to leave him alone now, but we labour under a collective family guilt that we should do more and continue to act as though he is still a 'normal' family-oriented man.

He always valued his independence, and now it seems he desires separateness. That might be okay for him, but what about us?

'You were supposed to come to the unit before you went to the doctors,' I continue down the line.

'Did I *promise* that?'

He's a cunning old bugger. Of course he didn't promise to meet me at the unit and go to lunch. Not even a vague indication that he might. Must have been wishful thinking on my part. 'It's just that I've been worried about you,' I say and immediately rue the whiny tone in my voice.

'Well, there you go,' he says like a self-centred teenager who has outwitted his mother.

'Right,' I say and slam down the phone. He won't give it another thought, and he won't ring back.

Now he'll be cocooned within his three-bedroom unit by the artificial lake, sitting in his large green reclining chair watching the end of an afternoon show on television – maybe *Wheel of Fortune* or some such thing – waiting for the early Channel Ten news. The vertical drapes will be closed to keep the last shafts of intrusive sunlight from entering, and apart from the flicker of the television, the only illumination will be a dull light from one of the table lamps.

Soon he'll pull himself upright with a grunt, straighten his back, and go to the kitchen to prepare his dinner: canned sliced peaches, half apricots, or pears, maybe with some ice cream or custard.

9

A Last Hurrah and a Diminishing World

Except for the occasional visits I make every six months or so, I know little of what his life Up North entails. His routine appears to continue as usual: going to lunch in town, to the Tumbulgum Tavern, to the more expensive eco resort/restaurant/art gallery at Treetops, or to the more basic Uki pub, sometimes with Eileen, sometimes not; flirting with the waitresses; going to the bank and avoiding, when possible, or forgetting his doctors' appointments; being asked to leave the golf club for unacceptable behaviour; and locking out family members who come to stay.

Then he's at it again. Down the main street of Murwillumbah he goes to chat up his solicitor's female paralegal, and up to the Gold Coast to see Dawn the real estate 'girl'. He's been organizing the sale of his Iluka unit and the purchase of a new luxurious pad in the Moroccan further up the glitzy strip, one of the new pseudo-Arabic buildings popping up along the coast, glistening white with fake domes and minarets and Ali Baba urns in the tiled foyers.

Why the hell in his early eighties Dad bothers buying the stunningly spacious unit facing the sea, I'll never know. Is he bored with life in the retirement village and thinks he'll rekindle his earlier relationship with Surfers Paradise and the ocean? Are the financial negotiations a way of feeling in control again? Is it – as his solicitor later suggests to us – just a way to spend time with the various women with whom he has to deal? Or does he feel he is coming to the end of things, and the Moroccan is his last hurrah?

*

On one of my visits, I drive up to Surfers with Dad and Eileen to spend five days in the new unit. There is no way I can get my father to myself; Eileen always tags along, and as much as I appreciate her friendship with him, I can barely contain myself as she blabbers away for the entire trip. By the time we pass Mermaid Beach, Dad can take it no longer and yells, 'For Christ's sake, woman, stop your inane prattling.'

Less than twenty-four hours after we arrive, she threatens to go back to Murwillumbah. Maybe they've had an argument I'm not privy to, but he tells her to go, and she packs her bags. He accompanies her to the bus station, pays for her fare, and waits to see her safely on the Murwillumbah bus. He returns to the unit sporting a vague smile that is difficult to interpret, and I am alone with him for the remainder of the week.

We don't do much, apart from driving out to the commercial hinterland to purchase a television. We don't talk much, either. Dad does his crossword, we go to lunch, and I devour a book a day. In the late afternoons, we sit on the wide sweeping balcony lulled by the waves, watching the sea change colour with the sunset and the moon appear above the horizon as we consume a bottle of Riesling. I wish it was him and Mum sitting here together clinking their drinks – she dressed in a long silk peacock green and blue dress, her white hair with a mauvish tint – watching the moon cast a wavering trail of brightness over the glassy Pacific.

Eventually, I leave him there and return to Sydney, imagining him relishing his luxurious solitude, the warm late October weather, and the sea. But within two weeks, he has the unit up for sale and has gone back to Murwillumbah. He is impossible to fathom.

The only thing he'd complained about to my knowledge was the garbage chute along the hall. Dad's hearing, though poor, is selective, and the banging of the lid, the clink and clank of tins, and the tinkle of glass bottles against its metal sides as they fell from floor to floor irritated him.

But perhaps it was something else, like the milling crowds and ear-splitting noise that erupted both day and night during October and November: roaring and snarling cars battling it out on a street circuit during the Indy 300 and the loutish and lawless behaviour of the teenage 'schoolies' engaged in a cultural rite of passage involving excessive use of alcohol, drugs and sex.

Could he have missed Eileen and the other women who daily passed his Mountain View unit, or the local waitresses perhaps? Or was it the serenity of the lake and the local bird life? For whatever reason, it was a costly mistake. He seems to have lost his ability to make competent business decisions, and he never again returns to the Gold Coast.

The circle of his life is growing smaller, although he still has his car and is able to move around the immediate environs of Murwillumbah. He has dinged and disposed of two cars already, although he never has the accident that I always fear. That is, not until he fails to take a curve – not near the cemetery, but among the cane fields near Tumbulgum, probably due to a combination of bad eyesight, slow reflexes, and grog. He is not hurt, and Eileen, who is with him, sustains only a minor injury, but that 2002 accident is the end of his lifelong love affair with cars and motors.

He loses his licence when the local GP provides evidence to the police concerning his eyesight and other conditions, and he is forced to rely on taxis to get to and from town, still adamant about not using the village bus.

I never hear him complain as he is inexorably squeezed into a smaller and smaller world. As far as I know, he just toughs it out and carries on with the routine rhythms of his restricted life.

*

It's a beautiful spring day in 2003 as I wind my way up Ewing Street to the 1939 red-brick building on the hill, a comforting sentinel to the inhabitants of the Tweed Valley, but for us, an ominous place, a harbinger of change.

The troops from Down South have answered a call from Eileen. 'You'll have to come, Greg's in the hospital. He's had a fall outside the RSL. Drunk, of course.'

Apparently, one minute he was eating roast lamb, potatoes, and pumpkin, followed by custard and jelly at the RSL, and the next he was propped up in a bed in Murwillumbah Hospital in a fugue of confusion, not knowing what happened after he escorted Eileen from the club's upstairs dining room. He'd had a fall all right, but he was not drunk. He was on the verge of kidney failure.

The main hospital building smells of chlorine, antibacterial soap, and the stale odour of years of hospital meals. The beige-walled corridors and the closed blinds keeping out the tropical sun produce a dirty-washing-water light. Whispered sounds break the tomb-like silence. I find him in an alcove off one of the verandas. There's a flicker of recognition.

'Have you come to take me home?' he asks.

'No, not yet, Dad.' I kiss him. His skin is cold despite the network of red capillaries in the craters of his cheeks. His face clouds over, but Eileen, who's been sitting beside him keeping guard, looks relieved to see me.

'I bought him some pyjamas,' she says and gets up. 'Well, I'd better be off. Got things to do. See you tomorrow, Greg.'

We thank her for calling us and staying with him. She scuttles out the door, brushing past Dr Hunter, Dad's GP, who scrutinises the chart hanging on the end of the bed.

'Greg's rather disoriented at the moment,' he says. 'Fairly common in these cases where urine banks up into the kidneys. He was in a bad way when they brought him in: rapid heart rate, low blood pressure, and dehydration. Do you know he recently had a short-term catheter inserted?'

'No, I didn't, but that's not unusual. He's never told us much. He's always been a rather stoic old bugger.'

'That may be, but it hasn't done him any good,' he says. 'I offered to get a nurse to check on him. Caring for a catheter is a lot of trouble. But he refused.'

Of course he did.

'He hasn't really cared for his health over the years, has he?' the doctor continues. 'Living on his own.'

'Well, no one forced him to move so far away,' I say. Then to counteract my terse response, I add, 'It's been difficult to help him.'

The question, of course, is: Did we really try hard enough?

There was a time when my sister rang him and he had to hang up: 'The pain's too bad,' he'd said. None of us had ever heard him complain before. And the time when his voice was strangely high-pitched, as if he'd inhaled helium from an inflated balloon. I did speak to his doctor once, but that was hardly much help. We would have needed to be on hand to really keep an eye on him. And that was exactly what he didn't want.

A rattle and squeak announces the arrival of the medication trolley, and Dr Hunter leaves to continue his rounds. A young plump-cheeked nurse – country-bred for sure – dispenses the pills and waits to be certain he swallows them.

'Dad doesn't seem too bad,' I say to the nurse, hopeful.

'Sometimes,' she whispers, 'but he doesn't seem to understand what happened to him and why he can't go home. For the last two mornings, he's taken off his pyjamas, put on his clothes, and packed his bag. We have to tell him,

"Not today, Greg," and then we undress him and put him back to bed. We've had to hide his clothes and suitcase.'

I tear up and turn away.

My sister has gone off to carry out various duties. My brother is at the solicitors with his 'power of attorney' label. Dad is dozing. I sit listening to the muffled thump of traffic in the distance and the chirrup of birds just beyond the sunny chinks in the blinds, guiltily thinking of excuses to leave.

A brusque female voice breaks into my thoughts. 'Which one are you?'

Looming over me is the stereotypical hospital matron: puffed-up-pigeon chest, thick ankles, and starchy attitude.

'Greg's eldest,' I say.

She squelches over to the bed on her hospital rubber-soled shoes and then beckons me to follow her out into the hallway. 'We need to talk about Greg's future.'

Here it comes.

'I suppose you know your father's been in here before with a urinary tract infection.'

No, I didn't bloody know.

'Once he's stabilised,' she continues, 'and the infection is under control, he's going to need a permanent catheter, and he's not up to living on his own. You'll have to organise alternative accommodation. He can't stay here; we don't have facilities for long-term stays.'

'Is he suffering dementia?' I ask.

She exhales loudly, and there's a ragged edge to her voice. 'According to his GP, he's already had some degree of dementia. Personally, I'd say he's had mild cognitive impairment for years. He's been a heavy drinker according to his records.' Her tone annoys me. 'And I'd guess, living on his own, he's had nutritional problems as well, particularly a lack of thiamine or Vitamin B1.'

'Will he improve?' I ask politely, although what I'd really like to do is answer her veiled reprimand.

'It's hard to say with someone of his age. His recent disorientation might only be a temporary condition, but I've contacted the Aged Care Assessment Team, and they should be able to give you some idea of the kind of managed care facility he'll need.'

Facility? Is that the official jargon now?

With that pronouncement, she turns and lumbers down the corridor, impatient to impose her authority elsewhere and to casually and coldly pronounce the words that will change other lives, just as ours have been irrevocably altered on that fragrant tropical morning.

10

Turning Points

Back in the motel, my eyes glaze over as I contemplate Dad's bleak future. Sadness morphs into despair and helplessness. I need a drink but have no energy to drive to the nearest bottle shop – can't even get off the motel bed to turn on the TV. I am gloomily preoccupied with what's ahead for him at this major turning point in his life and the decisions we will have to make as a family.

Against the background buzz of cheery chatter seeping through the wall of the adjacent motel room, my mind circles back to another accident, another club, another hospital, and another turning point.

I never really knew all the details when Mum broke her pelvis in January 1995, or if what I remember is correct. I think they were staying overnight on their boat tied up in the marina of the St George motorboat club on Kogarah Bay. Mum, unsteady on her feet – possibly tipsy – tripped and fell from the jetty into the dark oil-slicked water lapping at the barnacle-encrusted pylons. I would like to think that

Dad, with no time to think, dived in after her, but I really have no knowledge of how she was rescued.

That one moment changed their lives completely.

He accompanied her in the screaming ambulance to Kogarah Private Hospital and waited fearfully for the specialist's diagnosis and subsequent surgery. Try as I might, I can recall only vague details of visiting her. But I seem to remember her telling me when her nine-week stay was coming to an end that she would be a little sad to leave, as she had been so fussed over all the time. Did she have doubts at the time about Dad's ability to care for her, being as intolerant of sickness as he was?

But she needn't have worried. Dad was diligent in his role as carer, although I can't say how impatient or frustrated he became.

But who will care for *him*?

Me?

As difficult as it is to say: I don't think so.

It's not that I lack compassion for his situation, but caring for the sick just doesn't come naturally to me, and I doubt I could suspend my life to look after someone needing constant nursing and monitoring without feeling anger and resentment. I'm certain that if my father had any say in the matter, he would not want any of his children fussing over him, not want his daily loss of dignity paraded for all the family to see. No, he would rather pay a professional in a managed care facility to attend to his bodily needs.

Well, that's what I choose to believe, anyway. Selfish, maybe. Or just practical?

*

After Mum's accident in 1995, Dad sold his boat – his second great love – little knowing he would never again enjoy life out on the water at the helm of his own cruiser. He also put the waterfront house that he built in 1960, and its adjacent land, up for sale. The place was snapped up almost as soon as the sign went up. I can't say if he and Mum had already discussed selling, but the speed with which their entire lives were turned around surprised the family.

Of course he asked for no real help in packing up and disposing of the household effects, giving most of the big items to the Smith Family charity, keeping only what he thought he and Mum would need in the city unit, and offering the outdoor furniture, his extensive supply of power tools, the ride-on mower, and the pool equipment to the new owners. I'm sure many of the adult grandchildren would have loved the quirky objects they coveted as fashionably kitsch, but I suspect that stuff ended up in trendy inner-city junktique shops or in the apartments of first-home buyers.

I've often wondered what Mum thought about the speed with which her life changed. One day she was in the waterfront home she loved. Then she was on her back in hospital. And finally she was installed in a two-bedroom city unit. Maybe, at the time, highly medicated against the pain, she was pleased that he'd taken charge, relieved of the emotional trauma and physical effort of packing up her life. I've also wondered what Dad felt when he left their home for the last time. Perhaps there was a fleeting moment of sadness, but he was not one to dwell on the past; his mind, I'm sure, would have been firmly set on the future for him and his girl in the city unit.

But within a year, she went to sleep one night and never woke up, and he was faced with sorting what remained of their possessions all over again. I would have once suspected that when he had to dispose of two of his homes and the possessions of a lifetime, he carried it out with a cold practicality. But since my various intermittent stays with him Up North, I'm not so sure.

*

And now here I am in his unit by the lake going through *his* stuff, rummaging through the last seven years of his life, cataloguing his belongings and making a value judgment about what can be kept and what disposed of. It's an invasion of his precious privacy, the prelude to emptying his home, the place to which he will never return.

But I guess we all come to this at some point in our lives.

The only sound in the unit by the lake is the hum of the fridge and the enormous freezer that probably contains foodstuffs from the time he first moved in, the 'best used by' dates long since expired. I've opened the doors to allow a warm fresh breeze to circulate, and golden light pours into every room through windows no longer hidden behind rarely opened blinds.

Hugh, Dad's upstairs neighbour, raps on the front door, come to find out the latest news. I tell him that Dad won't be returning to his unit and that we'll have to take him Down South. The hospital has agreed to let him stay until we can find suitable accommodation.

Although there is no need, Hugh appears to want to justify something. 'Jean and I tried inviting him up for a meal now and then, and even offered several times to take him to the bowling club. He just didn't seem interested in socialising much. Kept pretty much to himself, I think.'

'I know,' I say with a lump in my throat.

Not wanting to dwell on the thought of the enclosed life Dad constructed for himself in the retirement village without Mum, I guide the conversation in a different direction, telling Hugh that we'll be coming and going over the next few weeks to empty the unit, and asking about the chances of selling quickly.

*

I go through the grey filing cabinet in his office, identifying those documents that are important and those no longer of use. Among the property contracts, chequebook stubs, and bank statements, there are a number of out-of-date black plastic-covered diaries, the ones he used to give out to customers at Christmas. I set aside anything to do with business or money or ownership of property for my brother to look into, as I am – or so various members of the family have reminded me over the years – financially challenged.

In one of the hanging sleeves of the file, I discover Dad's birth certificate, Mum's death certificate, and their marriage certificate. It occurs to me that the most important events in our lives are marked by these brief and impersonal one-page documents, carefully hidden away somewhere. Nothing more to show for these rites of passage than a few fragile and yellowish-grey pieces of paper that only now and then take on importance, often leading to a frantic search, trying to remember where the hell we put them for safekeeping.

Dad's faded birth certificate simply states that he was born on 17 March 1919, at home at 186 Mosley Road in the sub-district of St Martins in the County of Birmingham, to Annie Mary Carlson née Hicks (Birmingham) and Bertrand Aloysius Carlson, an engineer born in Redfern, Sydney. Could it have been just a coincidence that Dad, who worked with metal all his life and was something of an inventor, was born in a city known throughout the world since the Industrial Revolution for its innovation and metalworking?

Most of Dad's family tree beyond his parents is lost among the belching smokestacks of Birmingham, in the mists of Ireland, and along the rocky coastlines of Scandinavia. I know only the names of his paternal grandfather and grandmother: Oscar Carlson, a Swedish sea captain, and Hannah Kelly. Sitting on the floor in a rectangle of sunlight in his unit by the lake, I indulge myself by creating an imaginative scenario of the meeting of Oscar and Hannah.

It's the port of Liverpool, England. A commercial windjammer docks at Pier Head – or is it the Albert Dock? – crowded with masts and bustling with lighters and dockhands. The master of the ship supervises the unloading of the bulk cargo he's carried across the world: wool and grain from Australia, guano from the remote Pacific Islands, maybe lumber and coal from elsewhere. Before he returns to his family home in the Nordic enclave of the English city, he seeks a drink – or two, or more – in one of the seedy little taverns in the narrow streets behind the waterfront.

She's behind the bar. The young Irish lass beams at him, pleased at his safe return. He knows she's a member of one of the thousands of families who migrated to Liverpool in the wake of the Potato Famine – 'the Great Hunger', she calls it – a time of mass starvation, disease, and upheaval, a time of the great Irish scattering. He knows she has cousins in

New York and in Sydney. She knows he'll be rolling out the door soon, but he'll be back to see her several times before he sails away again.

Maybe Oscar marries Hannah, and takes her across the world on one of his trips. Maybe she becomes pregnant, and when the ship sails into Sydney Harbour, Oscar decides to settle down. Or perhaps he leaves her with her cousins in Redfern NSW – the inner-city suburb that was the first stop for migrants arriving in Sydney – while he's away, and that's where my grandfather, Bertrand Aloysius Carlson is born. Maybe … perhaps …

Stop!

I drag myself away from speculating and continue to focus on categorising pieces of paper and placing them in piles. Hidden away in an otherwise empty sleeve of Dad's files are two photographs. One is a sepia photograph showing three couples at a wartime wedding in the English port town of King's Lynn. There's no date on it, but judging from the British infantry uniforms and style of the women's dresses, I'd guess it was taken in the early 1940s. The other, snapped in 1933, is simply an image of Dad as a young teen sitting on a rock beside a lake or river staring into the water. To me, he appears rather melancholy, although with photos you can never tell; one captured moment could mean many different things.

I consider showing the photographs to Dad and getting some feedback, but he doesn't yet know that he will never be returning to his unit, and if he's any way lucid, he'll probably say, 'What the hell do you think you're bloody doing going through my personal things?'

When I visit later, he says, 'Good, you've come to take me home. Can you find my bag? The buggers have hidden it.'

'I'm sorry, Dad, but the doctor says you need more treatment and tests, so you'll have to stay here a little longer. Unfortunately, we have to go back to Sydney for a bit, but we'll be back in a few weeks. Eileen will keep you company. I've asked her to get you anything you need.'

I ramble on about nothing in particular: the pleasant nurses, the officious matron, the weather, until he falls asleep. I return to the motel, where I carefully wrap Mum's Lladro figurine in layers of tissue paper and place it inside my carry-on bag beside the large brown envelope containing the 'rite of passage' documents and the two photos.

||

Revelations at Coolangatta Airport

On the way to Coolangatta Airport in the Hertz hire car, I mull over Dad's birth certificate. Why had my grandfather Bertrand – a Sydney boy, a Redfern boy – gone to live in Birmingham before or during the First World War? He wasn't a soldier; he was an engineer.

I can't remember ever being told. Dad never appeared to have any real interest in his background: 'What's past is past,' he'd say, and the few times I tried digging into his early years, his responses were cursory. I was probably too distracted by my own life at the time to persist. But the need to know about his life seems more imperative now.

Maybe, like lots of young Australian men, my grandfather took off to the mother country and offered himself for the war effort by working in the vehicle and munitions factories of Birmingham. But it's hard to associate that young man with the Pop I knew: a small-time SP bookie in the 1950s, sitting in front of his wireless with a beer, his racing guide, and little black book.

I park the car, enter the shabby single-storey air terminal, and return the keys to the Hertz counter. The indicator board shows 'delayed' against my flight; at the check-in counter, I learn that the plane will be at least an hour late due to a severe electrical storm playing out all along the far north coast of NSW. For several minutes, I remain perfectly still and focus on inhaling deeply until my heart stops racing and my breathing returns to its normal rhythm. I queue to order a long black coffee and a soggy microwaved ham-and-cheese croissant and settle in to wait.

But I don't relax.

It's not just the storm. My relief at going home – even for a week or two – is tainted with the knowledge that my once independent father will never be the same again, and that those who are admitted to nursing homes rarely survive for long.

In an attempt to try concentrating on something other than the electrical storm and Dad's depressing future, I remove the envelope from my carry-on bag and slide out the wartime wedding photo I found in the bottom drawer of his files.

Although I'd never seen this photo before, I know the bridegroom's name is Robert and that he was killed in World War II not long after the photo was taken. He was my father's older half-brother, born out of wedlock to my grandmother; I have often wondered if it was just wartime, or whether Annie Mary was a loose woman. Just after she met Bertrand, she found herself pregnant once more. Fortunately, Bertrand married her one month before my father was born.

When Bertrand, Annie Mary, and eighteen-month-old Greg boarded a converted German warship in the second half of 1920, heading for Australia, Robert was not with them. I don't know if he had been fostered or adopted out before my grandparents met, or if my grandfather demanded his wife leave him behind, a price she had to pay for a better life. Whatever the case, I can't judge her abandonment – if that is what it was. It was another time, and I have no knowledge of the circumstances of her life. Perhaps she did what she thought was best for Robert, but she never saw him again, although she kept in touch with him until his death in the 1940s. She also maintained contact with his family until her own death.

I believe my grandmother lived with the gnawing loss of Robert all her life, and I often wondered if her remorse or sadness affected her relationship with Dad, who grew up an only child. Does a very young child sense such things? I don't know. Neither do I know if my grandmother ever spoke about what she had sacrificed as Dad grew older, filling him with undeserved guilt or hurt or anger.

Although I didn't know the story of Robert until 1965, my 'little nana' always seemed to me such a sad woman. As a child, it worried me that my mother never seemed to have a good word to say about her. My father didn't appear to like her very much either. I seem to remember a casual comment about her sharp tongue. Is it possible that such a trait is carried in the genes? Or is it an attribute picked up within the fabric of the family? It is possible she was not a very nice person, but I never saw any evidence of it and I always felt terribly sorry for her.

I guess Dad found the 1940s wedding photo when he was clearing out her home after she died. Maybe it was stored somewhere in an envelope or a box among her hats at the back of the wardrobe, or in the ebony-black cupboard with a pink silk lining – the only piece of her furniture I actually remember. I hope when he found it, he tried to look at things from a different perspective, to feel compassion for her, to accept who she was and what she'd done.

I am still lost in the past when an announcement blares through the departures hall: further delays. Members of a recently arrived group, bussed down from the Gold Coast, let out a collective groan. I double-check at the information desk, buy a glass of cheap white wine, and move to a seat close to the window overlooking the tarmac.

As I study the photo of Robert again, I wonder if Dad kept it as the only link he had with the half-brother he never knew. Did he feel any guilt about being the chosen one? Was that why – according to my mother – he wanted to call his firstborn Robert, if it were a boy? Perhaps he wanted to give his own Robert a secure and loving home.

I remove the other photo of Dad as a young teen, taken in 1933. Just a few years earlier, when he was 11 and attending a Sydney inner-city public school, his father took off to the alluvial gold fields of Bulolo in the highlands of New Guinea, leaving his wife and son behind in Sydney to cope alone.

Another abandonment?

Or am I being unfair?

After all, the Great Depression began the year Dad turned 10, and by 1932 a third of Australians were out of work. Perhaps Pop lost his job and was unable to pay the rent or mortgage. Maybe his apparent desertion was an unbearable decision.

There's no doubt working in New Guinea, without paying taxes, would have been preferable to joining the long queues each day outside the gates of the wharves on Sydney Harbour that became known as the 'Hungry Mile' – or 'taking to the track', becoming an itinerant worker moving from one country town or property to another. It might have been the only way my grandfather thought he could support his family.

But if my grandfather's departure to New Guinea was an important signpost in Dad's life, I suspect his mother's decision to follow her husband 'into the wilds' because she 'didn't trust Bert up there with those fuzzy-wuzzy women' was far more traumatic. Dad was only 13.

I'm sure that in the beginning, he lived with another family, and he did admit that she came back periodically. All the same, I imagine that at such a vital stage in his development, he would have been marked by that physical abandonment and lack of parental nourishment.

Despite his reluctance to talk about the past, this was the one story Dad told over and over, a tale that varied slightly with each retelling. His purpose, I suspect, was to show us how tough those teenage years were for him in comparison to our own, and how he had to tap into every shred of intelligence and determination he possessed to survive alone.

As I watch a mother on an adjacent seat trying to calm a tired and irritable toddler and a frustrated father admonishing his two restless teens, I look again at the photo of 14-year-old Greg, the boy left behind, the teen who one year later managed to find himself an apprenticeship and was living in a men's boarding house called the Winters in Drummoyne with a bunch of single male schoolteachers.

I try to imagine the emotional scars – well-hidden of course – he might have carried throughout his life.

Part 2

Down South

12

Room 22, South Wing

The desolate call of a bird matches my mood as I approach the ramp leading into a dim underground car park. The nursing home out on the frayed southern edge of the city is the last place I want to be on this sunny Sydney morning.

I climb the stairs to reception, sign in, and tap in the three-digit code. The lock on the security door clicks, and I enter South Wing, the air redolent with the smells of floor polish, disinfectant, and a faint hint of uric acid. But it's not the smell that makes me nauseous; it's the thought of seeing him sealed away in this place of collapsed bodies and minds, so dependent on others. Guilt seeps through me like an unsightly stain at what we've been forced to do.

Room 22 is an austere dorm for four men. There's an emaciated bundle occupying the bed at the far end, but I know it's not Dad; *his* name is on the empty bed closest to the door.

Despite his wealth, he's been reduced to the condition of a pauper due to the lack of nursing-home availability for men and the deadline we faced in finding a suitable one within reasonable distance of the family.

The tiny space allocated to him comprises a single bed with a striped blanket set against a bare wall, a lounge chair, and a grey side cupboard and wardrobe. The top drawer of the cabinet contains only a black comb with a stray grey hair, a worn toothbrush, and his leather wallet – once so full of notes, but empty now except for an old driver's licence. The second drawer contains a number of stained Y-fronts and flannel pyjamas, and his wardrobe is barely big enough for two jackets and several pairs of pants. Trying to hold back tears, I trace my finger over the gold- and red-embroidered pocket of the blue St George Motor Boat Club jacket he's had for well over fifteen years. I can see him still, with Mum, all those years ago, skippering his cruiser *Halcyon* out on Georges River and Botany Bay.

The smell of onions and the chink of cutlery coming from somewhere down the hall signals the start of lunch.

'If you're looking for Greg, he's in the common room.' It's a young nurse's aide. 'Come, I'll show you.' She places her hand on my arm, and I take heart from her gentle touch. I follow her down the corridor. 'He's in there over at the back,' she says, but she must sense my shock, for she adds, 'Don't be too sad. We'll look after him.'

There are more women than men, fragile huddled forms with vacant faces, some with the sad eyes of caged animals, remnants of once fine people. Compared to most, Dad, who is sitting in the far corner wearing the bright shirt I gave him last Christmas, appears so normal. But of course, he is no longer the determined, independent man he was just a few months ago, managing alone and going to lunch with

Eileen. My throat struggles as I wonder if this is all he has to look forward to – endless days among the anguished and agitated. And does he understand his situation? Does he think we've abandoned him?

I make my way between the aides busy calming and gently urging recalcitrant patients to the tables and tying bibs around their necks. Soon the feeding will begin. I draw up a chair beside him and kiss him on the cheek, but he's clutching at his left leg and appears a bit disturbed. The plastic bag connected to a yellow tube has slipped just below the hem of his trousers, and he needs attention before he eats.

When I alert a passing nurse and point, she nods impatiently.

Shit! What have we done to him? What's the point of living a long life if it's like this? Maybe it would have been better for Dad to have died in that fall down the Murwillumbah RSL steps.

*

After lunch, he takes a nap. It's the perfect time to make my escape, but instead I choose to stay until he wakes. I wander around the garden filling in time and wishing I'd brought a book. A neat little lady with a halo of fine silvery white hair – reminiscent somewhat of Mum – is sitting at a 'bus stop' waiting for a bus that will never come. She fiddles with an oversized purse and shakes her head distractedly. I sit down beside her, but not too close, for fear of startling her. She smells of something sweetly floral. 'It will be here soon,' she says in a reedy voice.

'Any time now,' I say, and we lapse into silence. A long ten minutes later, she struggles to her feet, smooths down her navy skirt, and with her bag looped over her left arm like the old Queen Mother wanders off on her bird legs, the sound of her shoes like sandpaper on the concrete path.

Back in Dad's room, I watch his flickering lids and wonder if he's dreaming of his girl. I hope, if he is, that it's not as she was when he last saw her, frail with osteoporosis. Better that it be when she was young: dark and slim in a long velvet gown the colour of Claret. I imagine her looking down at his sleeping form, listening to his laboured breaths, gently touching his sunken cheeks.

He stirs, mumbles something, and opens his watery eyes.

'You've come,' he says. 'I've been waiting.'

I hand him his glasses and help him sit up.

'Oh! It's you, Smellamy. I thought it was my girl.'

'No, Dad, just me.' My eyes prickle, but I'm relieved that in the foggy muddle of the past and present, he still remembers one of the weird nicknames he gave me as a small child.

'Let's go outside for a while,' I say. 'It's a lovely spring day.'

He shrugs off my hand as I try to help him regain his sense of balance and steady him as we leave Room 22. He's still not happy accepting help, and I experience a brief rush of anger.

At the security door, two female residents materialize out of nowhere and are lined up ready to 'escape'. Dad watches them, and I would dearly love to know what he's thinking. A nurse's aide hurries along the corridor. 'Back you come now, Elsie. Hold Gwen's hand.' She smiles. 'You have to be careful when you open the door, love. Some of them seem to have a sixth sense.' She sends her charges hobbling and shuffling back down the corridor.

'Like bloody children,' Dad says, and I wonder just how aware he is of his own situation.

The afternoon sun shafts into the courtyard, but my attempts at conversation are futile. Is he pissed off at what we've done? Does he feel betrayed, or does he understand that he needs a high level of care? I want to tell him I love him, but it's not an easy thing to do; he's never really been comfortable with shows of emotion from his children.

I'm anxious to be gone and hope he doesn't notice the number of times I glance at my watch. At three thirty, my planned time of departure to miss the peak-hour traffic, we return to South Wing, and I pass him over to one of the nurses.

'Come on, Greg,' she says, 'time for a cuppa?' I kiss his cheek and disappear as quickly as I can.

As I drive out of the car park, I imagine whizzing along General Holmes Drive towards the city with a fresh breeze blowing off Botany Bay, carrying with it the tangy smell of salt and the raucous squawking of gulls, and Neil Diamond's 'Cracklin' Rosie' blaring from the car stereo. But it isn't like that. I drive in silence, windows up, unaware of my surroundings, focussing instead on the prospect that in a few days I'll have to do this all again. I'm already despising myself for some of the excuses I know I'll come up with in the future.

13

Fellow Residents and a Family Day

Dad's been permitted to have his lunch in the sunny rec room in North Wing, but I'm not sure if the others around the table are any more coherent than those I saw on my first visit in South Wing.

A woman muttering to herself wanders aimlessly around the table until her husband manages to get her seated. Another fellow grinds his teeth noisily as a long-time friend and former carer tends to him. There's a skeleton of a man with skin as translucent as candle wax who just stares straight ahead. A woman, possibly his daughter, wipes some drool from the corners of his mouth. There are others around the large table who, no doubt, I'll get to know in the weeks ahead.

I take the empty seat beside Dad, and a fellow with badly knotted hands, who seems normal enough, introduces himself as John Gardner. I'm heartened somewhat for Dad's sake, but unfortunately he's not a resident. His wife, Mary, a stroke victim, is in a wheelchair. 'Brainstem,' he tells me. 'Left her locked in, unable to speak or move below the neck.'

'I'm so sorry,' I say, wondering if she can hear and understand.

'I really wanted to keep her at home, but my son said it was too much for me. Actually, it is rather difficult to get here every day now that my knees are playing up, but I'm sure Mary would notice if I didn't.'

I wonder if she would, or if that's what John wants to believe.

'Darl, help me with this,' Dad says, pointing to the bib in front of him. Suddenly I'm back in the days when my kids were babies, when some of the local mothers met for sporadic and much-needed adult conversation interspersed with the bottle, breast, mashed food, vomit, and wet or dirty nappies. As I fit the bib around his neck, I remember a more pleasant time when he donned a large vinyl one in an expensive seafood restaurant at Queensland's Sanctuary Cove, sucking the flesh from the nippers and legs of a large mud crab, the juice dribbling down his chin and collecting in the turned-up edge of the bib.

Eventually the food arrives: roast lamb, mashed potatoes, peas, and carrots swimming in a thin gravy. 'Looks pretty good, Dad,' I lie.

He cuts a small piece of the lamb, chews for a long time, and then takes the sinewy ball from his mouth and places it on the edge of his plate. 'A load of bloody crap.'

'C'mon, Greg, you need to eat.' It's one of the aides, and I sense him stiffening. Any kind of wheedling or cajoling would have once resulted in an angry outburst, and even now there's a flicker of his former self as he leans across the table and asks the gaunt guy opposite, 'What do you think, Jack? Will I kill her?'

Then the aide is at it again. 'Come on, love, eat your veggies.'

He pushes the largely untouched main course away like a petulant child, and I wonder if it's because he really doesn't like the food or if it's just his way of retaining some form of control.

'Pass me the dessert, darl,' he says.

He eats slowly, seeming to enjoy the sweetness of the stewed fruit and custard. He takes one sip of cordial from a plastic mug, but one sip only. Perhaps he's afraid his bag might leak if he has too much fluid. Or maybe he's pining for a nip of Johnnie Walker Black Label on the rocks, or a glass of white wine.

Opposite, Jack snuffles and then yawns widely, revealing the pallor of his tongue.

'Put your hand over your bloody mouth when you yawn, Jack,' Dad says. I smile and give silent thanks that there's something of his former self still there, but I am ashamed that he has to spend his days surrounded by such misery.

*

Thoughts about him buzz like a squadron of mosquitoes during the night, and I wake in a fog of exhaustion. I find my favourite old mug, pour a strong black coffee, and take it out to the balcony. In a corner, behind the potted olive tree planted to remind me of Greece and Italy, gnat-like insects hover around a small dead bird: limp grey-brown body with an empty eye socket. Its death saddens me, for it was a rare visitor to my balcony.

I tear off the front page of an old *Herald*, rummage around in a kitchen drawer for a plastic bag, and put on a rubber glove. But as I carefully place the tiny corpse in the middle of an article about another roadside bomb explosion in Iraq, there's a loud crack as shards of my coffee cup scatter across the terracotta tiles. Damn! Without warning, tears roll down my cheeks—but not for the loss of an avian visitor, the end of a favourite mug, or even the death and destruction in Iraq, as horrific as it is.

*

Far below my balcony, two local fire engines speed down Clarence Street, sirens blaring as they do several times a day, and against their high-pitched warning I almost miss the ringing phone. It's my sister-in-law. My solar plexus knots up. 'Is it Dad? Has something happened?'

'No, he's okay. Just rang to ask if you can do something. There's a family day next weekend, and the home wants a profile of Greg. Something brief, just the main points of his life, with a photo. Can you do it?'

'I guess I can do that,' I say, hoping she doesn't sense my reluctance at having to reduce my father's life to a few bullet points that won't reveal who he really was.

All day, memories of him come uninvited – unexpected things demanding to be noticed, some trivial and humorous, rising like a flock of birds; others like strange beasts pushing their way up from the muddy depths of my subconscious, unsettling me. Despite a whining headache, I have yet to search for a suitable photo to go with the pathetic skeleton of his life I am throwing together.

When it's finished, I email it to my sister-in-law to see what she thinks. 'Is it enough, will it do?'

'It's just right,' she communicates back.

No it's not. It reads like a bloody eulogy delivered by a minister who never knew him.

*

As I move around the walls of the home's reception area, reading brief accounts of lives almost spent, a single photo of a well-dressed and glamorous brunette with no accompanying life summary catches my attention. Her name is Harriet Smythe, and there's no mistaking her identity. It's the little woman at the bus stop. I am saddened at the thought that maybe she has no one to write her story, no one who cares for her, while seven of us – including my sister and brother-in-law from the country – have turned up for Dad on this stinking hot family day.

We sit under a green and white canvas awning with a cooler filled with several small bottles of white wine and a few beers, brought by my sister-in-law. Apparently, she tells me, Dad stole someone's beer from the communal fridge in the rec room. I didn't even know the residents were allowed alcohol. Maybe he did nick one, but I find it hard to believe because he would never have gone to anyone else's fridge without asking. Not even his children's. Not ever. And he'd raise hell if anyone dared go to his bar fridge without permission.

Our conversation becomes rather stilted. Dad seems to have withdrawn somewhat, and there's not enough wine or beer to go around to jolly us up a bit. For decades, we all reacted to him in our own particular way, picking up on his facial and body signals. We developed strategies for dealing with his feistiness, gave him a wide berth when the air in the room frizzed with his fiery energy, and usually knew when we could relax, when to pander to him, and when to keep quiet. But this new remote Dad unsettles us.

One of the nurses breaks the mood somewhat as she passes through the courtyard carrying a jug of water. 'Glad you could all come,' she says. 'Greg's so lucky to have you here. Some residents don't have any visitors today.' I want to ask her about Harriet Smythe, unable to get the woman out of my mind and not sure if my preoccupation is just that she's alone at the end of her life or that she reminds me so much of Mum. 'I wish I'd had a grandfather like Greg,' the nurse continues. 'He's always making jokes. It's a pleasure to look after him.'

Maybe that's our problem: we've become too serious with him, too solicitous of his welfare. Maybe we should be joking with him more often, teasing him a bit.

'You're one of the easy ones, aren't you, Greg?'

He smiles. One of the easy ones!

As she turns to go, I ask, 'Why is there just a photo and no story about the little lady who sits at the bus stop – Harriet Smythe?'

'I don't think she has any family,' the nurse says. 'At least no one comes to visit.' Tears threaten. 'We found that photo among her possessions. She's a lovely little thing; we do what we can.'

The nurse excuses herself, and the conversation turns to making a display of photos from our various collections to hang above Dad's bed. He shows no reaction, but we convince ourselves he'll be pleased. I suspect he won't really care one way or the other. To be honest, if we delved into our own motivations, we'd probably admit the display is a way of assuaging our guilt at depositing him in such a sterile environment.

The afternoon drags on endlessly. Various conversations, like ephemeral plants, sprout briefly, only to wilt and die as the afternoon sun casts long shadows into the courtyard. We retire to the rec room to have a cup of tea and biscuits, the prelude to our goodbyes. There's a sense of relief at the thought that our escape is close at hand. We have done our duty. I wonder if Dad will feel a similar lightness when we leave, as if relieved of a burden.

14

A Funny Old Geezer

Just ahead of me is a young male nurse with a cheery bounce in his step. 'Excuse me,' I call. He turns, and I see the name on his lapel. 'Craig, I'm looking for Dad … Greg … Greg Carlson.'

'Hi. Yes, he's out in the courtyard getting some sun.'

'Is he bare-chested?' I ask and laugh, although he wouldn't know of Dad's past habit of taking off his shirt whenever he got a chance.

He grins. 'No, I think he's fully dressed today. Your dad's such a funny old geezer, keeps me in stitches.'

I'm pleased, of course, but it occurs to me that Dad might be playing games, withdrawing when members of the family visit and then reverting to something of his former self when we're no longer there.

'Flirts with all the young nurses and aides,' he chuckles, but he must have read something in my expression because he quickly adds, 'They don't mind though, he's always a gentleman. It's good to have a lively one.'

There's no offence in his words. 'So you think Dad seems all right in here then, Craig?'

'He's fine. Forgets things sometimes, of course, but I think he likes being one of the few men among all these women.'

Always did, I think, remembering him waiting at the bar at the Motor Boat Club for Mum and the View Club ladies to finish their monthly meeting. Even though he thought some of her friends were 'as mad as cut snakes' and 'as silly as two-bob watches' – two of his favourite stock phrases – he'd buy them endless bottles of wine and shots of spirits with mixers. He was always the centre of attention.

'Just one more thing, Craig. You know the "specified behaviours" mentioned in the pamphlet we were given when he was first admitted. Does he exhibit any of them?'

'You mean calling out for help all the time? Or crying?'

'No, I certainly wouldn't expect him to ask for help. Or cry. I was thinking of some more provocative forms of behaviour.'

'You don't have to worry about your dad. He's one of the most normal people in this place. He's really no problem at all, believe me.' He smiles as if to reassure me. 'Sorry, gotta go, never enough time.'

Dad is where Craig said he was. He's sitting alone staring into the distance, and I'm reminded of the young melancholy boy sitting by the water in the photo from his file. I touch him gently on his arm so as not to startle him, and he returns from wherever he's been.

'Why are you here today?'

'I always come on a Thursday.'

'Do you?' He looks confused, turns his head away, and fixes his gaze on a point beyond me, as if expecting someone.

'Hi, Greg.' She's a pretty young thing: smooth oval face, large brown eyes, and hair pulled back with a blue scrunchie. She smiles and pats him on the shoulder. His eyes focus on her, and there's a change in his expression. 'Do I know you?' he says, his face more alive.

'Silly … it's Kylie.'

'Did I pick you up in a pub somewhere?' He gives her a roguish adolescent grin.

She turns to me. 'It's just a little game we play.'

Great!

She whispers something in his ear, and he lights up. 'See you later, love.'

As she disappears, his briefly animated expression fades, and his gaze slides away.

I take several deep breaths to release the frustration and wonder why the hell I bother.

*

I get off the bus in Military Road Mosman on Sydney's Lower North Shore, locate the cafe on Avenue Road, and order myself a coffee. I'm catching up with Helen, a friend from way back and a former geriatric nurse.

The waitress brings me a latte. 'Sorry, this is not mine. I ordered a soy flat white.' She looks around in confusion and returns it to the busy barista, who mouths his most colourful expletive. I'm not sure if it's for my benefit or hers. She returns, scowling, with the correct order. 'Some basic customer skills would be nice,' I say as Helen arrives.

I give her a quick peck, and she orders her cappuccino from the now sulky waitress who throws me a look that says *old bitch.*

We do the usual: What've you been up to? How's the family? Any trips lately? And so on. Then on to Dad's situation. 'So what's the problem? You sounded stressed over the phone. Are you having concerns about the nursing home?'

'No, that's okay … I think, although I'm only there for a few hours once a week, so it's really hard to know. But it's fairly new, only four years old.'

'Well, how does he look? Is he clean, does he seem well cared for?'

I tell her he's always clean and tidy, that they've had his hair cut and his eyes tested, he's seen the podiatrist and been assessed by a physiotherapist. 'Everyone seems to know his name, and they all seem to like him, but it's just that he's so impassive when we visit.'

'Well, that's better than being angry and disruptive.' She takes a few sips of her coffee. 'I assume he doesn't suffer from Sundowners Syndrome,' she adds, and then saves me from having to admit I've never heard of it. 'Some people with dementia and Alzheimer's become more confused and upset around sunset. It's a difficult time for the nurses. Bit of a mystery, really.'

'No, the staff members say he doesn't exhibit any challenging behaviour at all. He's one of the easy ones, they reckon.'

'Well, what's your problem then?'

'He flirts with the young nurses and aides.'

'Well, that's not so bad. Nursing home residents often take a liking to particular members of staff, and they're trained to deal with such things. Are you worried that he's got sexual urges?'

'For God's sake, Helen, I hadn't even thought of that. I suppose he could have urges, but he can hardly do anything with a catheter stuck up his penis, can he?'

The place is filling up with young Mosman mothers and their strollers, and we've attracted the attention of a bobbed blonde at the next table. Helen lowers her voice. 'People in nursing homes can have sexual needs like the rest of us, you know.'

Do I really want to hear about this?

She continues, 'Maybe in the future, the subject of elderly sex won't be so hush-hush, and there'll be some way to accommodate those who have the need.'

'Can't see any of the residents sitting around the lunch table with Dad needing a private space to shack up any time soon,' I laugh, looking sideways to see if the blonde is still straining to eavesdrop. She turns away quickly, and I whisper, 'He went to a clinic for erectile dysfunction once, not long after Mum died, but he told me some time later that he'd decided against the …'

I'm interrupted by a toddler at a nearby table who decides to throw a temper tantrum, screaming as he digs into the back of his stroller and takes out a Thomas the Tank Engine, a plastic trainer cup, a packet of Wipes, and his mother's wallet and throws them on the ground. His shrieks set off another indulged infant. Their mothers ignore them.

Helen pushes her chair back and stands. 'Oh, for heaven's sake, you young mothers,' her raised voice competing with the bawling, raging toddlers. 'Do something about your children!' They barely register her anger. 'Let's get out of here and go to the pub,' she says.

I negotiate my way through the prams, strollers, and toys to pay the bill. The young waitress hands me my change with another daggered look. I smile at her. 'Hope the rest of your day is better than it's been so far.' There's no point making a complaint to the manager.

'I'm really finding it hard to put up with little kids lately,' Helen says as we walk slowly up the road. Her leg appears to be bothering her.

'Frankly, I don't know how you ever did it – look after old people, I mean. I find it difficult enough seeing Dad once a week. I'm okay with the physical disabilities; it's the vacant and disconnected ones that depress me. And especially those who've suffered a stroke that has affected their ability to communicate.'

'That's the problem with you, Pam. Verbal communication has been your life, and when that's cut off, you probably don't know what to do.'

She's right of course.

The lounge bar in the pub is cool and relatively quiet. There are just three patrons: a couple exhibiting all the telltale signs of having an affair, and a young fellow hunched over his beer in a corner. We order two house whites and find a seat apart.

'Dementia sufferers may not understand what's being said,' Helen continues, 'but they retain their feelings and usually respond to other forms of communication.'

'Like what?'

'Like holding their hand for instance, looking them in the eyes, any form of tenderness and affection.'

That may be, but I can't see myself sitting for hours holding Dad's hand.

When she returns from getting us another round, she asks if there is anything else worrying me apart from Dad's flirting. 'He seems to be playing games. Doesn't talk much, sits in silence with members of the family, and yet …'

She interrupts. 'Old people become very self-centred, you know – less concerned with others and their feelings. Generally they don't seem to care about all the little stories we try to tell them to keep them occupied and entertained.'

'Yes, but that doesn't explain the way he becomes quite animated and playful with the staff. He doesn't seem to care if we're there or not.'

'Well, what was he like Up North after your mum died?'

'Much the same, I suppose. Wasn't too fussed if we visited or not, didn't really want us to stay with him, flirted with young women and joked with everyone else.'

'Well, there you go. Some people just can't cope with family anxiety and suffocating attention.'

'Helen, I wouldn't say we're exactly suffocating him with attention.'

'Yes, but there's a belief that people with dementia can read people's emotions and sense their impatience, frustration, anxiety – you know, all the things loved ones feel when they visit.'

Two men in paint-splattered white overalls push their way through a swinging door that links the pokie area and dump a pile of coins on the bar. 'One for the road?' the barman asks. There's a hearty laugh at some private joke between them. The infatuated couple gets up to leave.

'Be thankful,' Helen says. 'It doesn't sound as if your dad's dementia is overly severe yet. And just keep in mind that his silence isn't necessarily negative. Don't try to see meaning behind it.'

15

If Only I Didn't Have to Go

The weather has been foul. Clouds the colour of charcoal scud against an algae-green sky, and I can't think of anything worse than driving out to the southern edge of the city, trying to be caring, making conversation with people I don't know, and asking questions as if I'm interested.

By the time I leave the city via Cleveland Street, the traffic is snarling like a beast, with sounds of shrieking tyres and angry shouts. It's definitely a day for road rage. Up ahead, the line of cars has stalled, and a taxi driver has sneaked up on the inside and now wants me to let him in. 'Fuck you,' I mouth, gripping the wheel tightly and easing the car as close to the one in front as I can. On the radio, a shock jock rants on about a federal politician. Another station, and the usual media witch hunt continues. Who the hell appointed these dickheads as authorities on everything? Eventually, I find some light music to ease my irritability and try to prepare mentally for another visit with Dad. But what the hell kind of a daughter am I, grizzling over a one-day-a-week visit while all those good people out at the home look after him day after day?

By the time I reach the long sweep of Woronora Bridge, the sky has opened up and the rain is slanting off the windscreen, the wipers making no difference. I imagine skidding on the greasy road, doing a 360, and hurtling over the bridge railing into the gorge below, splattering onto rocks, a bloody mess of broken bone, torn flesh, and metal.

I've been thinking about death a lot lately – Dad's and my own. It's quite possible I could die before him, dead in an instant from an accident, a clot in the brain, or a blocked artery while he lingers on in a fog of dementia, his heart still beating strongly. It's unlikely, but it could happen. It was in this frame of mind recently that I read the death notices in the paper, looking for all those unfortunates who apparently died before their time.

I pull over and wait for the rain to ease. My gut clenches and my heart pumps rapidly as trucks and cars pass me, *swish … swish … swish*, with no reduction of speed, no respect for the weather conditions or the curves. I'm enveloped in the dark blue form of my Mazda on the shoulder of the road just before it curves over the Woronora River, and my breath has fogged up the windows so I can see nothing. Without sight, my imagination begins to play tricks. The rain batters against the glass and drums on the roof like someone desperate to get in out of the weather. I wind the window down a fraction to make sure, but the rain's unrelenting force hits me full in the face and I quickly close it again.

Inside my muggy cocoon, I wonder what it must it be like to be permanently fogged in, encased in a cotton-ball world of blurred images and undifferentiated sounds, just the occasional clear moment before it mists over again. Or even worse, being struck down with a stroke, like Mary, fully aware of what is going on yet unable to move or speak, the rage building up inside, the inability to communicate a living death.

I switch the heater to full, adjust the direction of the air to the fogged-up windscreen, and wait. There's a week-old newspaper on the passenger's seat. One of its front-page articles reports on the cooling of the property market, the steady decline in auctions (especially on the Gold Coast), the rate rise spooking the housing markets, and the possibility of bargains for those investors who are patient. Such an article would have once sparked Dad's interest, but not now. I locate the crossword page, tear it out, fold it as he used to, and place it in my bag. Just in case he's having one of his more lucid days.

The car shakes and the windows vibrate as a semi-trailer bores its way downhill. The clock on the dashboard shows 12.10 p.m. I'm late. I wind down the window, stick my head out to check the traffic behind me, ease the car out, and crawl down the hill.

By the time I reach the driveway of the nursing home, the sky is a sick yellow. The street gutters are overflowing, and a cascade of water churns down the home's steep driveway, over garden beds and into the underground car park.

Lunch is already underway, and I feel a creeping unease at the thought of the hours ahead. If only Dad's mind was still humming along.

According to the staff, he doesn't watch the television we had installed just beyond the end of his bed, thinking he might revert to his habit of the last seven years of watching the five o'clock news. The *Daily Telegraph*, specially delivered to him every morning, lies untouched on his narrow bed in Room 22, his magnifying glass hidden away in one of his drawers.

After several aborted attempts at conversation, I drag out the crossword. Yes, I know Helen said that I shouldn't worry about the silences, but the bloody virtue of silence is something I'm not real good at, and I'm determined to stimulate him.

'Dad, do you want to do the crossword with me?' No answer. I dig out a pencil from my bag. 'What's a monkey with a doglike face?' He's picking at something on the wooden table, and I allow the silence to tick on. John, on the other side with Mary, looks at me with what I interpret as empathy. I shrug my shoulders and try to refrain from sighing in frustration. 'Okay, it's a baboon,' I say and fill in 1 Across.

I do a few more and then, 'What about this one: "a period of time"? Starts with an *e*, three letters.' He appears to be watching a quivering shaft of sunlight on the opposite wall. Just give him time, I think as I listen to the ticks of the wall clock. Then, to entertain myself, I begin mentally listing all the time-related terms I can think of: time and place, time-consuming, time lapse, time limit, time out, time worn, time to come, badly timed, wasting time, 'bid time return', 'time's winged chariot hurrying near', 'The bird of Time has but a little way to fly', and …

The hands of the clock have barely moved. I write in 'era' for 4 Down and decide to try one more, scanning the clues for something that might elicit a response. *Yes!* 'Dad, do you remember the term for metal chips or filings?' I say, still seeing the piles of them accumulating beneath the lathes on his factory floor.

He gazes upward as if somewhere on the ceiling he might find the answer. 'No more bloody questions,' he says, fiddling with his hearing aids. He turns away and I enter 'swarf' in 21 Across.

'Thought he might still be interested,' I say to John. 'He used to do the crossword every day. I really don't know how you cope.'

'I just sit with Mary and talk occasionally. That's all I can do.'

After John takes Mary back to her room, I do the crossword myself. Every few minutes, although I know he's turned off his hearing aids, I make a comment about the drive over, the traffic on the bridge, the torrential rain, anything that comes to mind. His eyes are closed, and I wonder if he's asleep or just roaming in another world. It seems some days he's better than others.

There is no point hanging around.

16

An Intriguing Postcard

I am not yet prepared to give up. In the hope that Dad's long-term memory is still accessible, I've put aside a large black and white postcard he sent to Mum in 1940, plus a number of photos from the same period, for my next visit.

*

It was a summer night in 1938. A young man wearing cream slacks and a bottle-green jumper was singing with the band at a dance at Dee Why Surf Club, crooning recent hits like 'South of the Border Down Mexico Way' and 'You Must Have Been a Beautiful Baby'. The girl across the room with a gardenia in her dark hair was spending a weekend at the beach with older friends from Mick Simmons Sports Store in the city, where she worked as a stenographer. The young man's future was decided the moment he glimpsed her across that Surf Club room.

In 1939, he boarded a Handley Page 42E that carried four crew and twenty-four passengers and flew away – like his parents before him – to Bulolo in New Guinea, to work as a fitter and turner to save money for an engagement ring and to get married.

The postcard he sent to Mum at that time is simply addressed to Bloss, short for Blossom, one of his names for her in the early days. Looking back now, it seems a weird message to send to a fiancée:

> In the foreground is the new golf club house, plus baths and bath house. Behind the trees are situated the garages while higher up are the carpenters' shop and machine shop. This latter is the large building with the skylights in front of the crane. Beyond these again is the drome with a background of 'tailings' from the dredge. The 'tailings' take the form of bare rocks and will extend the full length of the valley, where dredgeable, eventually. Barely perceptible in the far background are houses on a private claim (whose owner is 16,000 pounds in debt). Also just discernible are some golfers on the drome. Cheers, Greg

'Cheers', not 'love'. No kisses. No 'I miss you'. No 'Can't wait to see you again' or 'Wish you were here'. Strange for someone who'd supposedly fallen in love – as he'd told us many times – with his dream woman at first sight.

*

After the cheery lunchtime brigade has cleared the table and the patients have gone their various ways, I place the card in front of Dad, anxious to see if it elicits any response.

'Do you recognise that place?' I ask and wait.

As if I have somehow willed it, he slides the postcard closer, but he makes no attempt to pick it up. The seconds tick by as he gazes at it. Finally his memory hooks onto something. 'It's New Guinea,' he says. 'Bulolo.'

Maybe it's a good day.

'You sent it to Mum in 1940.'

'During ...' He pauses as if on the brink of a question. 'The Japs.'

'Yes. It was before the Japanese invaded New Guinea. You went there to work for the Bulolo Dredging Company, to make money to get married. Would you like me to read it?'

'Not particularly.'

I try to hide my frustration. 'Okay, well, what about these?'

I lay out three photos: one of him holding a metre-high wooden twenty-first birthday key with a bunch of men with whom he shared the house in Bulolo, another of him in the lush Morobe Rainforest, and one astride a large Norton motorbike.

I remember him telling us that each weekend, he'd ride along the Bulolo Valley for motorcycle meetings at Wau, which because of its elevation at 1,080 metres became a hill station for many of the expats working in New Guinea.

He picks up the photo of the Norton and examines it closely. 'Is that me?'

It's amazing how my emotions morph so quickly from one thing to another. There are tears now trembling on the edge of my lashes as I say how handsome he was. And he was: muscular and blonde, so young and alive.

He carefully puts it in the pocket of his shirt, and there's a tender pull on my heart.

I push a larger photo towards him. He's bare-chested, sunning himself stretched out in a deck chair on board a Burns Philp trader. It's about a year before the Japanese attacked Pearl Harbour, and he's returning to Sydney to marry Mum.

'Haze and I are gonna go across the Pacific on one of these,' he says, and it's almost more than I can bear to hear him still holding onto his dream of crossing the Pacific in a cargo ship with Mum, dead now for seven years.

*

They were married in St James Presbyterian Church at Burwood soon after he returned from New Guinea in 1941. And eleven months later, on a humid Sydney summer day in February 1942, I entered the world at a little cottage hospital called Woodley in Hurstville. My birth coincided with a new phase of WWII when the Japanese decided to bomb Darwin, torpedo the NSW coast, and send midget submarines into Sydney harbour.

There's an old Spanish proverb that says, 'The lucky man has a daughter as his first child', but I suspect Dad may have hoped for a son first, a boy called Robert. All the same, judging from the softness and pride in his young face as he gazes out from the little black and white shots I have in my possession, he certainly doesn't look like a man who was disappointed with the gender of his firstborn.

We lived briefly in a flat at Bronte in Sydney's east, and each day he pedalled his bicycle – the Norton having been left behind in New Guinea – to and from Camperdown, where he spent his days in the Gothic Revival building in the grounds of Sydney University that housed National Standard Laboratories. I don't know what work he did there, but it was a centre of scientific excellence, and because the research conducted by the laboratory was of importance to the war effort, he was never called up to serve.

While his old stomping ground in New Guinea was invaded and the town of Wau destroyed in 1943, Dad, at the age of 24, bought a house in Blakehurst, a southern Sydney suburb where he spent the next fifty-two years of his life.

17

I Lived Here Once Long Ago

I have returned to the street of my childhood looking for the double-fronted dark brick house on the large elongated block that Dad bought in 1943, and where I lived between the ages of one and twelve. I hope in doing so that I might reconnect with the place that shaped who I later became and discover something of my father as a young man and of our early relationship.

The hill, as we once called it, is not really a hill at all. Maybe it just seemed that way to little legs pumping up and down to and from school. Grey or beige-rendered houses, now butted up against one another on the Terry Street 'hill', have replaced the simple suburban homes of my childhood friends. They are monstrous houses that have been built by people who seem to care more about internal than external space, whose children watch TV or play video and computer games and who probably don't build cubby houses in the bush, even where a remnant of bushland still survives. The Terry Street of *my* childhood was a place of spacious blocks, a tangle of bush, and warm human exchanges.

I guess I had expected Number 18 to be still there in some updated form, but its disappearance along with Numbers 16, 14, and 12 – all now villa complexes – fills me with an overwhelming sense of loss. I have a niggling feeling that perhaps in trying to relive some of my childhood memories, I might lose that childhood forever.

The only evidence that our family home was once halfway down the street is the little fibro house that belonged to our next-door neighbours, the ones with the chook yard out the back. It hasn't changed much, except it's now covered with weatherboard. And there's only one house I recognise on the other side of the street: a dilapidated 1920s cottage, waiting, I suppose, for someone to die so that an upwardly mobile young couple can renovate it or greedy developers can get their earth-moving equipment onto the block.

I park in front of our house that no longer exists and try to remember what it was like – to see beyond the modern pale brick villas with their trendy gardens full of ornamental grasses and pebbles. But I have no control over which memories slide in from the past, some singly, others in batches. Most are out of sequence.

In my mind's eye I see my father Out the Front, as we called it – the area demarcated from Out the Back by a sweet-pea-covered lattice on one side and an old two-metre metal gate on the other. He's broad-shouldered and stripped to the waist, whistling as he tinkers with his pride and joy: a little Austin or Morris or Vauxhall or Holden. It doesn't matter which; the scenario was always the same, the car parked on the concrete driveway in front of the fibro garage for some form of weekend maintenance. If I could open the doors of that garage and let you glimpse inside, you would see the evidence of not only a practical man but one who was obsessively organised and tidy. Every tool and piece of equipment was carefully stowed in its correct place, every rope or hose wound neatly, buckets stacked, benches clear and ready for action, not burdened under the crap usually found in most men's storage sheds or garages.

Few people had cars then, but we were lucky – not because we were rich, but because Dad was a 'donk' man. He loved anything with a motor in it. The car we were proudest of was the first Holden he bought: a brand new 1951 Guinea Gold FX Holden, ACH 767. It was a metallic brown-gold colour that apparently was the result of a mistake in the paint formula at the factory. Dad loved it; we loved it. General Motors didn't produce many, so we always attracted attention wherever we went.

Out the Front was well cared for: geometric shaped areas of lawn, concrete paths laid out by Dad, and the gardens my young mother planted – full of pansies, marigolds, zinnias, gerberas, and dahlias – that provided fresh flowers for the cut-glass vases around the house. But because Dad preferred flowering shrubs, Mum also made a no-fuss shrub garden beside the fence on the high side: pink and purple fuchsia ballerinas, orange Chinese lanterns, velvet purple lasiander, one shrub with creamy blossoms that sizzled with bees, and the pink oleander with its poisonous white milk. She made only one mistake as far as Dad was concerned: the cotoneaster. We waged war with its red and orange berries, crushing them on his precious concrete paths, defacing his pristine driveway with hideous red stains.

I can also 'see' myself Out the Front, balancing on the edge of the covered electricity box near the fence. As a child,

I used it as a launch pad, propelling myself far across the neat trapezoid of kikuyu lawn that was often filled with patches of bindii. If I complained about the bindis poking from my soles and heels like the spikes in running shoes Dad would yell, 'Stop that whingeing and don't be such a sook. Go inside and put your sandals on. Make it quick. And when you come back, I want those tar stains off the front mudguard of the car. Later you can carry that pile of weeds Down the Back for your mother.'

I don't know how long I've been standing in front of the house that was once ours, but I am pulled away from my memories by a female voice and the crunching of footsteps on gravel.

'Excuse me, is there something I can help you with?'

Number 18 morphs back to its modern villa form. A baby-boomer-aged woman dressed in golf gear stands with arms crossed and feet apart as if ready to confront me. She's obviously suspicious of the stranger standing staring into her driveway.

'I lived here once a long time ago,' I say. 'I was just trying to remember what it was like.' But she has no interest in my past and simply turns and walks towards her garage, dismissing me.

I leave my car and walk up the hill. There's a small, sturdy, freckled-faced girl with amber hair climbing the hill with me – the child I once was. On her back is a brown satchel filled with freshly sharpened pencils in a wooden slide-top pencil case, a ruler painted with scenes of the Blue Mountains, a soft white eraser not yet blackened with use, and a paint box with indentations in the lid for mixing new and exciting colours like Crimson Lake and Indigo. There's also a thin exercise book covered in brown paper with a picture cut from an old Christmas card and her lunch in a recycled paper bag. At the crest, she leaves me, and halfway down the other side joins up with other children from the street.

Retracing my steps, I stop at the house where my four girlfriends lived with their two brothers – Lionel, the 18-year-old who Dad employed in his back workshop with the second-hand lathe, and Billy, who famously once blew a tooth out of his nose. In the tea tree scrub behind their house, we built an igloo-shaped hideout filled with needles from scraggly casuarinas and moss collected from a dripping rock shelf. And we had concerts on their front veranda.

Sounds from long ago ring in my head: the raspy calls of 'bottle-o' and 'rabbit-o', the former coming down the hill in his cart drawn by a heavy rust-coloured draught horse dropping dollops of steaming manure on the road, the latter with his pink-skinned carcasses. In those days, the milkman filled our enamel billies left on the doorstep before the sun came up; the garrulous greengrocer and baker in their truck and van flirted and joked with the young housewives; the dapper Fuller Brush man periodically went from door to door with his fibre suitcase filled with brushes of all sorts; and the Rawleigh's man peddled his salves and medicines.

I continue on my walk down the street of my childhood, testing my memory as I pass each renovated or rebuilt house, trying to recall the families who lived in each one during the first twelve years of my life. I've been doing a lot of that lately: testing my memory. But I wonder if what I'm remembering is really as it was; memories are such elusive, unstable, and fragmentary things, shifting and changing over time.

The little shop on King George's Road where we did our grocery shopping has long since gone. It's now painted an aubergine colour and is the Jaanz School of Song and Dance, creating stars of the future. How I wish there'd been a dance school when I was growing up.

I dig deep for memory fragments of that iconic corner store: a squeaking wire mesh door opening into a dim interior; hessian bags full of sugar, flour, and potatoes lying in one corner; large tins of Arnotts Famous Biscuits with their colourful parrot logo; jars of black and white humbugs and pink and white peppermint lollies; Mrs Saunders's blood-red fingernails, with crescent moons unpainted, clicking and clacking against tins and containers; and Mr Saunders looking over the specs balanced on the end of his nose.

In my mind, I am returning from the shop with a string bag filled with supplies to make chocolate crackles and fairy bread for my sister's birthday. Then *he* is there – the local six-year-old thug – barring my way, pushing and shoving, pulling the bows from my hair, the groceries scattering across the pavement.

'What's wrong with you?' Dad demands when I push open the back door, my face streaked with dirty tears, my legs and arms grazed, and minus my hair ribbons. But worse, without the Cadbury's cocoa, the Kellogg's Rice Bubbles, and the packet of Hundreds and Thousands.

'Jimmy Seal,' I sniff.

'Well, I think it's time we sorted that young bully out,' he says as he dabs red mercurochrome on my scratches. 'And stop squealing like a stuck pig.'

Sorting the young bully out meant nightly boxing lessons and instructions, such as 'The next time he tries anything, give him a good right jab and an upper cut.'

And I did just that the next time he confronted me. The muscles in my right arm tensed as I squeezed my little fist into a ball, launched it at Jimmy Seal's chin, and landed one just as Dad had shown me. I sucked my sore knuckles triumphantly as my tormenter ran off down the street howling like a baby. That was the end of him. But I've often wondered if that incident set in place a certain pugnacious tendency, as I was never bullied again as far as I can remember. Of course, as I grew older, I replaced physical defence with verbal thrusts.

Terry Street and my young father have begun to reveal themselves to me, but I don't know if the language I've used to describe them has transformed the memories I've grabbed onto. I dare say some of my recollections could be called into question.

18

A Laundry and a Concrete Slab

The bush adjacent to the nursing home is alive with sounds, but in the courtyard Dad and I sit in silence. Near my feet, a line of ants disappears through a crack in the base of a brick wall, and I gently disrupt their file and watch their reaction, wishing I could simply nudge Dad and get a response.

He watches me with his washed-out grey-blue eyes and a remote smile. I note he's not wearing his hearing aids. Periodically, he'd remove them because they drove him nuts, he said, when people were talking all at once, reminding me of the song from *Midnight Cowboy*: 'Everybody's talking at me, can't hear a word they're sayin'.' I wonder if that was how Dad felt for the last seven years. Is perhaps some of his so-called dementia simply deafness?

'Where are your hearing aids, Dad?' I ask. He doesn't answer. 'Dad,' I lean in closer, 'where are your hearing aids?'

'Took the bloody things out. Probably been stolen by now. They steal all my things, you know.'

'Who does?'

He shrugs.

'Listen, I'll be back soon,' I say and pat him on the knee. 'I'll go check.' He doesn't seem to care.

There are no earpieces in any of his drawers, and a jumper is missing from his wardrobe. Neither is there any sign of the new batch of pristine Y-fronts my sister-in-law bought several days before. The undies could be in the wash, I suppose, but surely not all of them.

The humid laundry, smelling of astringent industrial-strength detergent and bleach, is huge and empty. Endless washing machines and dryers are labouring away at various stages in their cycles, a twenty-four-hour operation, and I am reminded of the warm soapy smell in a laundry from long ago.

In my memory, my mother is standing there in her work dress, struggling to lift wet sheets from the copper with a bleached wooden pole, making sure they don't drag on the floor as she transfers them to the concrete tubs to put them through the ringer. The steam has raised little drops of perspiration on her forehead and above her top lip. I am there too, leaning against the laundry door, barely able to see through the wire screen that covers its upper half, talking to my imaginary friends Lalie Lalie and Bassie. Dad is doing something on the concrete slab he laid at the bottom of the laundry steps.

My father loved concrete. He wasn't against grass, he just did whatever he thought was practical, a concrete-around-the-edges kind of man. 'Makes everything easier to look after,' he'd say.

Some of my earliest memories revolve around the laundry door and that concrete slab in our Terry Street home.

I have a vague recollection of our dog Tiger, of me crying, and of Dad with a hose in his hand, standing on the cement square. I'm not sure if he did anything more than turn the hose on Tiger, who maybe took a nip at someone. He wasn't an animal hater – we always had dogs – but neither was he soppy about them. One day the dog disappeared, apparently given to one of the itinerants who hawked their stuff from door to door. True or not, I don't know.

I remember him hosing down the slab of concrete, making it a clean slate so he could show me how to draw up a hopscotch court with its 'Safe', 'Home', and 'Rest' squares, and then watching me hopping on one foot, to make sure I didn't touch a line, miss a square, or lose my balance.

Once, he drew a perfect chalk circle, and when he'd finished, he handed me a cotton bag with a drawstring filled with colourful cat's eyes, aggies, and alleys, a number of shooters, and lots of mibs. I was *so* proud – the only girl in the street with her own marbles. Over the weeks, he showed me how to knuckle down, lag, and shoot. I practised and practised, and eventually the green-eyed boy monsters in the street invited me to play in the dirt circle in the scrub opposite. They thought they could beat me in a game of 'for keeps' and take off with my precious stock. They couldn't, but obviously they lived in hope, for I was allowed to join their marble gang.

Delving deeper into my memories, I hear the slapping of a skipping rope on the concrete and a girl counting, the clucking of bantams from next door, and my father saying, 'Put that rope away and go and feed the chooks. And make sure you mix their feed exactly the way I showed you.'

Watching the antics of the spotted bantams from our side of the fence was fun, and I had offered to feed them while our neighbours were away, but I didn't like their squawking fuss when I tried to shoo them off their nests to get the warm eggs. And I was frightened of the cranky rooster. Then there was the slimy green and cream mess that filled the rubber grooves on the soles of my shoes that I had to clean off afterwards – goo that made me heave.

'Can't I do it later?' I pleaded

'You'll do it *now*. Not when it suits *you*,' Dad said, holding back the loose palings to reveal the gap we used for going in and out of next door. 'And mind that old fella doesn't peck you,' he warned. 'Here, just in case.' He handed me a stick. 'About time they took an axe to him,' I heard him say as I disappeared through the hole in the fence.

I am drawn back to the present by a voice saying, 'You okay, love?'

'Just waiting for the dryers and washing machines to finish so I can find some of Dad's missing clothes,' I say.

'Try those containers on the table. They're labelled. So are all the clothes. If your dad's things are not in his box, have a look through the others. They sometimes get put in the wrong ones.'

I find a shrunken shirt in his container, a shirt I had given him before he left Murwillumbah. Then, like a voyeur, I rifle through the stained belongings of others as the washing machines jerk and whir on spin, and the dryers rumble to the cool-down phase. I check each as it stops.

My hunt for the missing new underpants is unsuccessful, but the forgotten memories that emerged from the swirling steam of the home's laundry have stirred up a need to look further into my childhood relationship with Dad.

19

Out the Back, Down the Back, and Inside

During the 1940s and early 1950s, most of our lives were spent on the street, in the adjacent bush, and running freely in and out of neighbourhood backyards. Out the Back was the more ordered, 'proper' part of our backyard that included the already mentioned concrete slab, the proverbial brick shithouse with its pan toilet, the Hills Hoist at the centre of a star of concrete paths, and a cubby house on the edge of the wilderness of Down the Back.

The outside dunny was made from the same bricks as the house and was surrounded by mint gardens to hide any smell that the antiseptic poured into the pan didn't cloak. It had a wooden slatted door, square sheets cut from old telephone books or newspapers attached by string to a nail in the wall, and occasional spiderwebs in the rafters. Going to the outdoor lav at night freaked us out as young kids; we never knew what creatures would be crawling over its walls and roof.

Dan Dan the lavatory man – that outcast, that untouchable in navy singlet – came once a week in the very early hours of the morning. He appeared and disappeared before the heat of the day attracted flies and accentuated the odour that followed him and his multi-doored cart. He arrived no matter what the weather, even in the pouring rain. The night before he was due, Dad ordered us to clear away any toys carelessly left around and to make sure there were no obstructions in his way. No one wanted a trail of our family excrement leading all the way to the front gate.

Dad had replaced the old wire clothesline and wooden prop with a new Hills Hoist in 1948, the first one in the neighbourhood to do so, because he loved anything new on the market, especially if it was made of metal and was practical. So he didn't mind paying £11 for it, twice the average weekly wage. I think he saw something of himself in Lance Hill, who began making the prototype rotary lines in the wash shed of his Adelaide home when he returned from World War II. That rotary line was the perfect piece of gym equipment for us in those days, so long as Dad never caught us hanging upside down like monkeys, swinging around with our heads mere inches from the ground. It also became a plaything for our frenzied, yapping blue heeler pup, Digger, on washing days.

The cubby house Dad built on the edge of Out the Back and Down the Back had a timber table, benches, cupboards, and two hinged mirrors. Its raked corrugated iron roof, partially hidden under the prolific choko and passion-fruit vines that trailed from the weathered, paling side fence, gave it the appearance of something out of a fairy tale. It became the clubhouse for our neighbourhood secret society.

Out the Back was also where we held the periodic street fêtes. Dad made the trestle tables, and the mothers provided colourful tablecloths and baskets of iced patticakes, scones, real Anzac biscuits, and butterfly cakes filled with mock cream. The kids, in fancy dress, ready for their concert, arranged and sold everything from home-made icy lemonade, tiny raffia rafts of coconut ice, and sticky toffees to the endless crocheted, knitted, and sewn doilies, teapot cosies, and doll's clothes.

In contrast to the order of Out the Back, Down the Back was a little piece of wilderness: a place of flowering plants gone wild, thistles, and longish grass that Dad occasionally took a scythe to. I don't remember any concrete down there, but there were dirt paths and damped-down areas where we often hid – oblivious to the dangers of bugs and spiders – during our games of hide-and-seek and cowboys-and-Indians. There was a permanent circle of ash from our previous year's Empire Day bonfire, built by everyone in the street but always carefully monitored by Dad from the sidelines, hose at the ready. It was on that burnt site that we dumped the garden rubbish and grass clippings from Out the Front and Out the Back.

Down the Back led, via a gate in a paling fence, to a wire-enclosed clay tennis court, its net never stretched tight no matter how much we tried rotating its winding handle. I can't say who owned the court; it just seemed to be there for the use of the locals. To one side was a rather dilapidated shed with a wooden table and benches where the adult neighbours gathered on a Sunday to gossip over afternoon tea while waiting for their turn at mixed doubles. The air was filled with the *slap, pop, slap* of the balls, the occasional dispute over an umpire call, and a 'damn' as a misplaced ball disappeared over the wire enclosure. Dust from the red clay court coated everyone's white sandshoes, shorts, and tennis dresses. In my mind, it is always summer, although it probably wasn't. Terry Street was a real community back then. It was a much simpler time, at least for children, and I suspect for adults too.

*

Not long after my parents moved to Terry Street, Dad decided he wanted to be his own boss, live on his own terms, and never have to answer to anyone else again – except for the bank manager, of course. He converted a back room into a small workshop, making tools on a second-hand lathe, literally working on the 'smell of an oily rag' to support his family. In those days, we went to bed with the odour of cutting fluid in our nostrils and the hum of the lathe as urgent orders were rushed through the night.

There are no photos of Inside, so I have to rely solely on my memories to build up a collage of bits and pieces. I mentally move through the laundry with its smell of wet clothes and Persil towards the workshop with its clang of metal on metal. Dad was always there behind the closed door in his greasy grey King Gee overalls. With him would have been Lionel, the youth from across the street, and Harry, one of his tennis friends yelling at each other above the whir, clank, and jangle of toolmaking.

In my mind, I continue towards the comforting sound of a wireless and what I remember of the kitchen, the throbbing heart of our home: a gathering place in the days before TV, before family and rumpus rooms, before kids disappeared into their own cubicles, doors firmly locked against invading parents and siblings, wiring themselves for sound or connected to cyberspace chat rooms.

Most days there would have been the delicious smell of a rabbit or lamb stew on the stovetop; once a week, a roast in the oven. There were rarely any fancy sauces with our meals because Dad said they disguised the natural flavour and hid 'crook' meat.

Green kitchen walls come to mind from somewhere. Maybe they were green and cream like the canisters and handles of the kitchen equipment. But it's the kitchen sink I remember most clearly, that deep white enamel bowl where I learnt to wash up properly. To Dad, 'properly' meant washing in the right order, starting with the glasses, followed by the cutlery and cups and so on. And beware if we ever left the steel wool lying on the edge of the sink.

He had rules for everything. There was to be no talking while we ate; no eating with our mouths open; no noise when we swallowed or slurping our drinks; no elbows on the table; no eating like the 'Yanks'; no grasping the cutlery up near the head; no yawning without our hands over our mouths; no burping without an 'excuse me'. Needless to say, we were urged to say 'please' and 'thank you' until they became second nature, and we were expected to put the knife and fork together when we finished eating; ask permission to leave the table; push our chairs in; fold up our serviettes and replace them neatly in the serviette holders … the list was endless.

My parents were often stretching limited family resources back then. I remember Dad on the back step resoling two pairs of school shoes while Mum darned a sock, the heel pulled tight over her wooden darning mushroom. She was always darning, dying, letting down, letting out, and taking in our clothes, as well as making new ones on the Singer sewing machine she received as an engagement present. I loved watching the way the bobbin moved up and down and the stitches nibbled away at the fabric, faster and faster the harder she pressed against the lever with her knee. She dyed our shoes different colours and transformed her own into gold or silver for an important occasion.

After tea was always Mum's time. In my memory, I can still see her fiddling with the dials of the Bakelite radio, a signal for us to keep quiet – she wanted to listen to her favourite quiz show. But I wouldn't be put off, continuing the questioning I began earlier: 'What if a baby was never given a name? Would that mean it didn't really exist?' She ignored me as she concentrated on adjusting the reception. 'Do we need a name to be a real person?' I rattled on. "If I had no name, who would I be?'

Dad had come in from his workshop. 'For crying out loud, Pam, just put a sock in it for a while. Leave your mother alone. Where do you get all these questions from anyway?'

He went to the kitchen sink, washed his hands twice, took a bottle of stout from a cupboard, and poured a schooner-sized glass of the black stuff with its creamy head. He handed it to Mum. He was always trying to fatten her up; he thought she was too skinny. Then he opened the fridge to get himself a beer.

'Who's been at the chocolate?' he demanded. He turned around and glared at my sister and me. 'Well … which one of you is the thief?' A family block of chocolate was the occasional Friday night treat he doled out sparingly over the course of a few days.

'Not me,' I said.

'Not me,' said my younger sister.

'Get over here.' We stood side by side while he pulled back the foil, carelessly replaced to hide the crime. There were three segments missing. 'Now who did it?'

No answer.

'There's a clue here,' he said. 'Look. A tooth mark.'

And there it was indeed: the indentation of a front tooth. He stood in front of each of us and jabbed his forefinger several times into the soft part of our chests. 'Own up and take responsibility.' No response. 'All right, go to your room, both of you,' he said. We were each given extra chores around the house for the following week.

On the rare occasions that my parents went out socially, my maternal grandmother came to look after us. She'd sit in the lounge room with its circular mirror and black wall phone, sipping tea from a pink floral china cup and crocheting delicate lace edges onto squares of linen, making the handkerchiefs she gave as presents. My mother would finally appear in a swirl of colour – a transformed Cinderella – dressed either in a long swishing taffeta dress with the scalloped neckline, or a gown of soft claret velvet draping to the floor, with long sleeves and a high neck to hide her jutty collarbone.

'You ready, darl?' Dad would ask, standing in the doorway dressed in his dinner suit. He'd help her with a small white furry cape that just covered her shoulders and twirl her around, singing in his best Perry Como voice. Then they would disappear, out through the frosted front door with its green dimpled diamond insert, leaving the house empty of colour and music.

Around dawn, my sister and I would sneak out to the kitchen in expectation of the goodies left on the table from the night before. Sometimes there were paper plates containing soggy, crust-less sandwiches, and segments of passion-fruit-coated sponge or rich creamy chocolate, the icing clinging to the serviette. Occasionally, if we were lucky, there might be lollies in little cardboard baskets like the leftovers from a child's birthday party.

One night, Dad and Mum had a visitor in the lounge room. Always curious to learn some forbidden piece of information, I slid out of bed and tiptoed as far as the hall near the front door. I didn't really understand the snatches of conversation that reached me except for the words *death* and *accident*, mentioned several times. Someone got up and I scurried back into my room, but when I heard Dad say, 'Want a beer, Chris?' and go to the kitchen, I took up my eavesdropping position in the shadows once more. The stranger's voice asked Mum how old she was, and he mentioned a few large numbers. Then, as if to punish me for listening, I heard Dad say 'shit', which he had once told me was the 'worst word in the English language'. My eavesdropping had introduced me to the world of 'do as I say, not do as I do', and for days I avoided him. I never heard him swear again until I was much older, when he started using curses like 'bloody' and 'bugger' for effect.

It was a Christmas morning, and in the soft light of our front bedroom with the casement windows, I saw the identical shapes standing beside my bed and that of my sister. They were wooden cradles, made by Dad for the china baby dolls with their blue glass eyes and horsehair eyelashes. I decided I didn't like that painted smiling china head; I didn't like it at all and would never play with it, and I didn't like the fact that I had received the same present as my younger sister. I'm not sure whether my later mantra of 'that's so unfair' began on that Christmas morning or not, but I do know that I registered a feeling along those lines. Mum had dressed the dolls in identical clothes. Everything was the same except for the colour of the cradle liners and the dolls' clothes. My sister's were pink and mine were blue. But wasn't blue for boys?

And speaking of boys: the arrival of my brother in 1951 was the signal for a change in our Terry Street life. Mum was preoccupied with a new baby – a Peter, not a Robert – and Dad at 32 had moved out of his back-room workshop to make way for his son and into his new factory, built in a neighbouring street.

20

A Floppy Blue Hat and a Concert

I am earlier than usual, and in the fluorescent glare of South Wing, there's nothing but a humming silence. It appears deserted. Dad's not in his room, but there's something lying on his pillow. It's a photo of him in a multicoloured bow tie and a ridiculous hat, a silly blue floppy thing that accentuates his red bulbous nose and makes him look like a geriatric clown. I would seriously like to tear it up. My thumbs and forefingers twitch as I imagine ripping through the silly hat and right down the middle of his nose.

'Oh. I see you found the photo. Good, isn't it?' It's a nurse trailing after an old man with a befuddled sadness in his face who has shambled into the room. 'He's quite a character, your father. Perhaps someone can buy a frame, and we'll put it on his cabinet.'

You want us to put a snapshot of an old clown in pride of place? I don't think so.

'Most of the residents are in the hall being entertained,' she continues. 'You can join them if you want. Come on

Billy.' She gently takes the old man by the elbow and guides him away.

I stay where I am and look up at the visual record we arranged above his bed. He's looking down at me, a confident man full of himself, at the helm of one of his cruisers, wearing a captain's cap. And there's a much earlier image of him in a helmet, getting into a racing go-cart he built himself, the determination to win on his face. There are others of him relaxing on holidays, sporting snappy little straw hats balanced jauntily on the back of his head and a variety of jockey caps pulled down to protect his eyes.

My gaze drops once more to the snapshot in my right hand. There's a hint of a vacant grin. It's hideous. But why do I care so much about it? And what's so bad about a stupid picture of him in a funny hat anyway? After all, he wears a bib three times a day, has a catheter stuck up his penis, and has his leaking bag emptied by nurse's aides. He's already lost his dignity, as far as I'm concerned. So what's so bad about a stupid picture of him in a funny hat?

Please don't let me end up like this, I think, and then I realise that maybe my reaction to the photo is not about Dad at all but about me. A future wizened-up old thing, dressed up, maybe with a funny hat, vacantly grinning into a camera, my children embarrassed for me.

I return the photo to his pillow, leave South Wing, and peep into the hall where the concert is in full swing. Like most nursing home and retirement village-type entertainment, it has lots of colour and movement. The master of ceremonies, a spry gentleman with a thin moustache and sleeked-back hair – a car salesman-type except for his bright green silky shirt – is playing a piano accordion and singing. His female sidekick has a stretched smile on her face and is all swirling frills and flounces. She is tap-dancing – click, tap, and twirl, click, tap, and twirl – and as he finishes his song on a surprisingly high note, trying to impress his unresponsive audience, she makes one last energetic pirouette.

He places his instrument on the floor and launches into a series of jokes. 'Did you hear the one about the 60-year-old man with the 60-year-old wife who wished for a wife thirty years younger, then zap, he was 90?' There's a smattering of laughter, mostly from the staff scattered among the residents.

Dad is in the middle row between two women. I can't see his face to gauge whether he's enjoying himself, but if he's in any way lucid, I'm sure he'll be critical of the performers. Probably thinking 'What a bunch of bloody ratbags.' And if there's a singalong, he won't join in; he's never been one of the herd, although he sang often at home and had a good crooning voice. I can hear him now singing one of his old favourites, 'The Darktown Strutters Ball'.

'Why don't you go in, Pam?' Craig has come up behind me.

'No thanks; I think I'll sit in the courtyard until it's over.'

*

A childhood memory glides through into the present. I am 8, dressed as a bluebell – cotton bodice and curling crêpe-paper petals. We are all bluebells and daffodils, readying ourselves in a tableau and waiting for the curtain to go up at Rockdale Town Hall. From my position in centre front, I turn to check that everything behind me is okay, but one of the girls isn't in the right place. I rush back, push her into the correct spot, and am barely back at the front when the worn red velvet curtain is jerkily raised.

Short bursts of sound are followed by applause. The nursing home concert has come to an end, and I return to North Wing, where the first person I see is Harriet, her old face glowing with the hint of a smile fluttering at the edge of her mouth. She looks like a child just come from a party. I try to catch her eye, but she is off somewhere else, perhaps doing something she once loved, and as she passes by me I'm sure I hear a soft trilling sound.

Dad is alongside a woman with a squeaky walking frame, moving slowly, favouring his left leg. His companion rattles her frame as a signal, and he steps aside to allow her to go into a side room. He sees me and gives a nod.

'How was the concert? It sounded quite lively.'

'Never seen or heard such crap. Big-noted himself.' I assume he's referring to the piano accordion player in his green silk shirt.

'Dad, what's wrong with your left leg?'

'Swollen big toe.'

I wonder if his gout has returned; he's had attacks of this so-called 'rich man's disease' previously. 'We'll get the doctor to have a look at it.'

'Whatever.'

'Ready for lunch?'

'You tell me.'

Despite a flicker of anger, I try keeping my face as neutral as possible and help him settle at the table. I don't bother talking to him over lunch. Instead, I focus on the sun creeping across the far wall, and on Jack's daughter tracing her finger around the lip of a glass of water as she tells the woman next to her how far she has to travel from the Hills District to visit her father. And I think about Mum. She wouldn't have been so critical of the concert, and she certainly wouldn't have let someone take a photo of her in a funny hat that would have messed up her fine hair. But then, if she'd lost her mind, she probably wouldn't have cared.

21

A Place of Diamond-Bright Days

I need a break to clear my head before heading back into the city. I've been mentally beating myself up since leaving the nursing home about my lack of compassion for Dad's pain and irritability. On an impulse, I turn off the Princes Highway at the sign to Carss Park and make my way down to 'Carssy', as we used to call the bush reserve with its netted swimming pool on the inlet in Kogarah Bay. It's a place where I spent many of the diamond-bright days of my childhood, and I only have to think of the name to hear the screams and laughter of kids from the past, taste the salt on my lips, and smell the eucalyptus fragrance of the bush.

I have a very early memory of that place. Well, maybe it's not my own memory; after all, I was only three and a half. Perhaps I embroidered a story my parents told me once. Apparently, I'd managed to climb the two-metre lattice screen that separated Out the Back from Out the Front. A woman on her front veranda thought she saw me disappearing into a side street and rushed to find my parents. The neighbours joined in the search, but by the time they questioned people all along Terry Street and Heath Road, I had already crossed the Princes Highway, the 'big road' as I called it. It wasn't really a busy highway then, but I had never crossed it alone; my hand was always grasped tightly by Mum or Dad. Perhaps I had in my mind a place I'd been to before, a place of swings and seesaws and sand.

Dad must have suspected that was where I was headed; he rushed home, got his pushbike, and took off. As he entered the bush track that led to Carss Park, he slowed and called out to one of the Chinese market gardeners who pointed, and Dad pedalled for his life, and for mine.

I had taken off my shoes, and was skipping up and down on the edge of the water when he found me. I looked up and smiled, but he threw his pushbike to one side and pulled me roughly to my feet. 'Don't you *ever* scare your mother like that again.' I didn't understand why he was so angry. I thought he had come to push me on the swings.

If that was the first time I went off the beaten track, it was certainly not the last.

After that episode, Dad took me on frequent bike rides to 'Carssy'. He'd pedal up streets that started with a B – Benwerrin, Borghah, Bunyala – and then circle down to the water and do a lap of the park. I seem to remember enjoying those times alone with him, but then on one such excursion, I lost concentration and my left foot slipped in between the revolving spokes of the wheel. He caught me just before I fell; carefully released my foot; lowered me, screaming, to the ground; and tore a strip of cotton from the bottom of his shirt to stem the blood. I can't remember the pain of that injury, how we got home, what Mum's reaction was, or if they took me to the doctor, but I still have a faded scar on my left ankle.

*

Carss Park doesn't seem to have changed too much. The nineteenth-century Carss' Cottage is still there as I might have expected, and the giant Moreton Bay figs with their serpentine roots clinging to the rocks that once seemed so high. The bubbler set in sandstone is still there. I press it, and the water squirts in my face just as it did when I was a child.

The Lifesaving Hall doesn't appear to have changed either, and as I stand in front of it, I'm transported more than fifty years into the past to one of the monthly school socials. I can still hear the music drifting from its windows, and see the parents inside twirling and swaying to the Jazz Waltz while the kids sit and watch.

I remember Dad asking me to partner him in the Pride of Erin, but I knew I mustn't tread on his shoes as we twirled or he wouldn't ask me again. When the music stopped, he returned me to where all the kids were sitting and gave me a gentlemanly bow – making my friends giggle – and then he led Mum out onto the floor for the Gypsy Tap. Everyone in the room got up for the Progressive Barn Dance. The kids mixed happily with each other's parents as they passed from one partner to the next, but were highly embarrassed when they came to one of their classmates of the opposite sex. Sometime during the night, a supper of curried-egg-and-lettuce and ham-and-pickle sandwiches, lamingtons, and Bushells tea was prepared and served by the mothers. The social, as we called it, ended with both adults and children joining in the hokey-pokey.

From the moment I started Blakehurst Primary School – that little cluster of classrooms on the rocky outcrop among the Angophoras, Cootamundra wattles, and peppercorn trees – Dad, who was only 27, became involved in the Parents and Citizens Association. Not only was he a man deeply committed to his family, but he also believed in helping out at school working bees and organising social functions.

The tracks in the bush behind the Hall are now overgrown, and the silence is broken only by the occasional gunshot crack of a falling branch, the rustling of insects, and the cry of a bird. The bush seems to be waiting … waiting once more for the whoops of those children from long ago, cooeeing, piercing the air with their eucalyptus-leaf whistles, throwing aged woody banksia cones at one another, hanging from branches, and running wild.

I walk out to the point so that I am directly in line with the net strung across the inlet. The oyster-pocked stone steps that led down into the water, once covered in tiny crabs at low tide, are now fenced off. There are no children stroking furiously to see who can reach the net first, and no one scrambling up it to stand on the barnacle-covered grey wooden posts that held it in place. No screams as they push each other off the old pontoon, long gone I suspect because it would be regarded as too dangerous in our now safety-conscious society with litigious parents. I don't remember anyone ever getting injured (although it probably happened), only happy carefree kids swimming all through the summer.

Back on the main path that once led to the old kiosk, showers, and toilets – also gone now – a woman runs past me with no flicker of acknowledgement. Near the swings and seesaws, a Chinese grandmother supervising a toddler glances up, her eyes watchful as she moves towards the child and hovers. I smile, but she doesn't. I catch the smell of Chinese cooking and notice two bowls of something on a nearby picnic table.

The shadows are lengthening, but there's one more thing to do before I leave. On the little crescent of beach, I take off my shoes, wiggle my toes in the sand, and skip along the edge of the water – a 61-year-old woman reliving a child's adventure. Just as well; there's no one around, except for the suspicious Chinese woman.

Carrying my shoes, I head for the car, but as I pass an unused BBQ, I catch the smell of meat sizzling on a hotplate. Then I see him in a Hawaiian shirt and a silly cloth hat a little like the one he was wearing in the hideous nursing home photo. He's cooking 'snags' and rissoles for one of the school functions. I watch my young father for a while involved in his community service, and then, with a farewell flourish of my hand, turn and leave that place of long ago, regretting that I was so irritated with him earlier.

22

Oysters and Prawns at a Sutherland Hotel

For the past week, the sky outside my city unit has been congested with dirty clouds; inside, it's hot and heavy. The only sounds apart from the throb of traffic are the whir of my cheap plastic fan in the lounge room and a struggling air conditioner on the balcony of an adjacent unit. While my body sags, as if rung out like an old dishrag, my mind turns to the nursing home residents and poor John struggling on arthritic legs to get there to see Mary by lunchtime.

It's Thursday again, and although I'd rather be staying home, I gear myself up for the long drive out to Illawong. Well, that's not strictly true; it's only about forty-five minutes, but it seems longer because of the disconnection that faces me at the other end.

I really need to find an activity to share with him, one that he might enjoy and which will enable me to go home with a certain sense of satisfaction.

*

I ask him if he'd like some oysters or prawns for lunch. 'Whatever you like, darl.'

Although he doesn't appear too fussed one way or the other, *I* want to get away from the home. The nurse on duty says he can have a glass of beer or wine but reminds me about his bag, so I decide to take him only as far as a hotel in Sutherland with seafood on the menu.

I consider asking him if he wants to go visit Mum at Woronora Cemetery just up the road from the pub, but I know what he'll say: 'What would I want to do that for? She's not there.' So I don't suggest it. Besides, I can't remember exactly where her plaque is; I haven't been there since she was cremated. And I really have no wish to go anyway. Like Dad, I don't see the point.

Unfortunately, the pub is a bit depressing: white plastic furniture, fluorescent lights that would drain the life out of even the most robust of patrons, and tables that need a good wipe down. I'm embarrassed to have brought him to such a place and would like to say 'Let's get the hell out of here', but I don't want to agitate him, so we settle at a table that's relatively clean. Next time, I'll take him somewhere near the water.

I order oysters for him and prawn cutlets for me. I hate oysters. Have done since I was ten, when he asked if I'd like to try one. Although I'd wanted to appear grown-up, I was unsure of the things in the long narrow bottle that looked like specimens from a medical laboratory. When I closed my mouth around the lump of slimy flesh, I almost gagged. Unable to swallow it, I pushed it up against my cheek until I was able to leave the room and spit it into the garden among the pansies. Now I can only stomach oysters if they are heavily disguised with a mornay or bacon and Worcestershire sauce. For me, they are not worth the cost.

Dad sits as still as a statue on the white plastic chair, the fluorescent light accentuating the hollows in his cheeks. I ask him twice whether he wants a beer or a wine. 'Wine, love,' he says, but when I return with it, he takes one mouthful and pulls a face. I have to admit it's a bit dry.

'Leave it, Dad, I'll get you something sweeter.' Fortunately, the pub still stocks Moselle, although it's well and truly passé these days. He sips it slowly, and when the oysters and prawns arrive, he looks carefully at the plate in front of him. 'Is there something wrong, Dad?'

'From the river?' he asks.

I tell him I don't think so, as a mysterious disease called QX wiped out the Sydney rock oyster business in the Georges River in 1995.

'From Oyster Bills?'

'No, Oyster Bills closed a long time ago,' I say.

While he seems relatively lucid, I try reconnecting him to other times. 'Remember our Christmas holidays when you used to collect oysters and place them on a heated piece of iron and wait for them to pop open, slurping them down straight off the hotplate?'

He smiles but doesn't add anything. Then between his second and third oyster, he asks, 'Durras?'

'Yes, Durras Lake.'

Originally we spent our summer holidays with some of the Terry Street crowd at Werri Beach, an idyllic spot, its beach and lake below the pines of Gerringong village with a backdrop of green rolling hills. But the year my brother was born and I was 9, Dad decided to change our holiday destination to Durras Lake. It was much further down the southern NSW coast, a relatively hidden place then, with both lake and long stretches of pristine beach surrounded by bushland.

I ask if he can recall taking us prawning, but he just continues eating his oysters.

'Come on kids, get a move on,' I hear him calling all those years ago. 'Let's go see what the prawns are doing.' We'd follow him through the dark, managing the hurricane lamp and the scoop nets while he strode ahead carrying a large kerosene tin and the big net. My sister and I would stand together up to our waists in the lake, holding one end of the net while he moved out to shoulder-deep, waiting for the prawns to make their dash to the open sea. Mum was always ready for us with a large pot filled with brine boiling away on an open fire. We'd sit around the fire until late eating cooked prawns followed by chunks of rum-soaked Christmas cake. The leftover prawns were stored in the icebox for the following day. For me, prawns and fresh bread and butter remain forever the taste of summer.

When I hear Dad cough, I drag myself back from that primitive campsite at North Durras to the dreary pub bistro. He's slumped in his chair twiddling the stem of the wine glass. It's time to leave.

'I'll just go and pay the bill,' I say. His hand goes straight to the fob pocket of his trousers – a lifetime's habit – searching for the folded notes he always kept there. It's empty now. 'Don't worry, Dad. It's my treat this time.'

23

Getting Back to Basics

No matter where I am, the *ark ark* of a crow and the summer smell of the bush always evokes those Durras Lake holidays: endless days of surfing; messing about in a patched inflatable dinghy or canoeing around the upper reaches of the lake; hiking along fire trails; fishing at dusk; and prawning at night. Every day was a new adventure.

The narrow dirt track that led from the Princes Highway to North Durras – for we were North rather than South Durras people – wound through a forest of eucalypts scattered with primeval cycads. It was in a bad way, full of axle-busting ruts and ridges, but Dad was a great driver and able to handle the soft dust that, during a dry spell, lightly coated the adjacent trees and scrub and provided a warning of cars ahead. After rain, the track was far more dangerous, with greasy sucking mud and pools of water. A driver's miscalculation could have a skidding car wrapped around a tree. Not Dad, though. He relished the constant twisting and turning of the wheel and changing of gears. And that was with a fully loaded trailer on the back.

When we arrived at the tiny settlement with its few private holiday shacks, we headed into the area leased by old man Lovell and his wife. Just as we were North Durras people, we were also loyal Lovell's campers, for there was another camp and cottage site next door called Bundilla.

Lovell's had around six cabins with tank water and hole-in-the-ground dunnies strung along a small rise on the edge of the lake. The rest of the property – blistered with cow pats from a small number of grazing jersey cows – was available for camping. Except for the choice spots on the lake flat and 'the point' beyond the last cabin, it seems, looking back, to have been a rather casual arrangement: find a spot in the open or under a tree, shoo off the cows and their clouds of flies, clear the spot of the khaki cow pats, and erect the tent.

There was a less-than-adequate general store, but Mr Lovell in his worn overalls and battered utility negotiated the rutted bush track several times a week to pick up supplies no matter what the weather. When he returned, the tray of his ute was filled with aluminium milk cans; boxes of bread, eggs, and bacon; meat for BBQs; day-old newspapers; beers; and special treats for us kids, usually tins of condensed milk, liquorice straps, or bags of boiled lollies.

Dad could have gone himself, but he said, 'We're not paying camping fees for nothing. We're on a holiday, not a shopping expedition.'

Maybe twice in four weeks, he packed us all up and took us into Bateman's Bay sprawling along the Clyde River, or upriver via a ferry to the Steampacket Hotel at Neligen.

Camping was a cheap holiday, but more importantly, it was one of Dad's ways of teaching us how to live simply and sensibly – 'It's time you girls learnt to get back to basics.' He was fond of saying things like, 'Go easy on the tank water. Have a dip in the lake instead,' even though our hair stood on end thick with sand and salt.

I can still hear him calling for the repair kit, and see him sitting astride a faded green and yellow fold-up stool, hunched over, threading a huge needle with coarse thread. Fifteen minutes earlier he had chased a curious Jersey cow out of the tent with a broom. The poor animal panicked and tore a hole in the mottled white fabric of one of the walls.

Memory fragments float into my mind in no particular order: the heavy canvas tent with large centre pole, four side poles, lace-up corners, and an extension made by Dad to house the trailer in which my sister and I slept ... Dad yelling 'You've laid out the wrong-sized tent pegs and tangled the ropes' and expecting us to lift the heavy mattress out of the trailer each morning to get rid of the little grainy circles of sand that collected around the buttons ... simmering midday heat and lazy yellow afternoons ... an old blanket spread in the shade of a tree ... calm preoccupied animals, the smell of fresh manure and canvas baking in the sun, drowsy flies, an unremitting cicada chorus, and the distant suck of the surf ... Dad lying on his back reading *The Phantom*, one of our Christmas-only supply of comics, Mum halfway through the *Australian Women's Weekly*, my brother asleep, and my sister and I busily cataloguing our collection of shells, seeds, and pebbles, cicada husks, iridescent Christmas beetle carcases, cuttlefish, and driftwood in all shapes and sizes ...

Occasionally, Dad would spear-fish at low tide with the older teenagers around the rocky outcrop just off the mouth of the lake while we younger kids chased crabs, collected periwinkles, squashed the brown cunji to make it squirt water from its siphons, and dug for pippis. Dad had shown us how to wait until the water receded, keep our legs together, and then twist and wiggle our feet into the wet sand until we felt the edge of the shell. We'd found a colony of them, and when our bucket was only quarter-filled, he called out, 'That's enough. If we collect too many and we don't use them all for bait, we'll have to throw them away. Just a waste.'

Dad always had a list of holiday rules – for our own good, he said – particularly when it came to surfing along unpatrolled beaches. We let him tell us each day which part of the beach was the safest and followed his instructions about no surfing after four o'clock in the afternoon: sharks' feeding time. We listened attentively when he taught us how to recognise an ocean rip and how to handle ourselves if we were caught in one, but I imagine we complained when we were not allowed rubber surf o'planes, like the other kids, until we had mastered body surfing and the ability to make it all the way into the beach 'under our own steam'.

But aren't rules meant to be broken?

A pounding dumper pummelled my body, forced my head into the hard gritty sand, and discarded me in the shallows like a dead fish or a piece of battered driftwood. I'd tempted fate and Dad's anger by moving to a part of the beach where the waves were bigger. As punishment, I was not allowed in the surf for four days, forced to sit in the shade against the beach cliff minding everyone's towels, sun hats, glasses, and bags.

Dad's survival program included more than just water safety. He warned us against eating the poisonous bright red fleshy seeds of the female burrawangs. Hundreds of those cycads that once dominated the world about 200 million years ago were scattered throughout the bush. He explained how to avoid being bitten by a snake on one of our many forays along the fire trails searching for the elusive white tree orchid, and what to do if we *were* bitten. He showed us how to get rid of ticks so that they didn't release their poison into our bloodstream. But when we emerged screaming from the bush covered in bloodsucking leaches, he just laughed. 'They're harmless; stop being sooks.'

From time to time, the long, lazy days of those summer holidays, suddenly separated into something exciting, and dramatic.

Once, a southerly buster howling at night through the eucalypts, snapped two of the tent's side poles. It was hard to hear Dad's instructions above the gale and pounding surf as he yelled for us to release the guy ropes, and drop the remaining poles so that the canvas fell over our camp gear. We were forced to sit on the corners of the tent in the dark, waiting for the wind to drop.

Another time, a bushfire roared somewhere in the state forest between the camp and the highway. Days of white heat had finally sparked the bush, and a strong westerly wind was driving the fire towards the coast. The sky had turned a dirty orange. 'Don't underestimate nature; things can change suddenly,' Dad said as he bustled us, with all the other campers, to the lake. We lowered ourselves up to our necks in the tepid water and placed wet handkerchiefs on our heads as ash drifted down and eucalypts exploded. And there we stayed until the wind changed in our favour.

And sometimes it was torrential rain for days on end.

I can't remember exactly when Dad changed from camping to hiring one of the basic wooden cabins at Durras, but I suspect he got sick of packing up a wet tent and then having to erect it again when we got home to keep it from getting mouldy. Nothing much changed on those holidays, though: it was still as basic as ever, and we were still learning how to get back to fundamentals. Mum was still making piles of sandwiches and keeping the water boiling for the prawns, but cards and board games replaced comics, and on lazy hot days we listened to the Davis Cup and cricket on our portable battery-powered wireless. Instead of searching for flotsam thrown up on the beach, my sister and I went looking for boys.

Not once in all the years we were growing up did we ever miss our four-week summer holiday.

24

Moving On

My childhood was not idyllic by any means, but large chunks of it have always remained close to my heart, and I believe that my young father's expectations – his script, if you like – activated my curious, naturally competitive and independent personality.

But changes were on the way.

A photograph that I like to think represents my rite of passage into a bigger world shows me standing beside the front gate in my new high school uniform: blue pleated serge tunic, blazer, gloves, lisle stockings, and dark blue velour hat. It must have been the winter after I turned 12 when Dad thought I was finally responsible enough to own a watch. The little silver thing, with ruby-like jewels marking the five-minute intervals, is clear in the picture, glinting against my navy blue glove. It is quite possibly the last photo of me in the street of my childhood, taken the year of Queen Elizabeth's first visit to Australia.

Dad began spending more time in the small engineering factory he'd built at 23 Heath Road before the birth of my brother. It was originally 10 metres deep before he extended it twice and eventually built right through to 992 King Georges Road. It was there that he really transformed himself into a man of steel. And it was about the same time that I wrote in my journal how I thought he saw *me* as a raw piece of metal that could be shaped on a lathe, ground until all rough edges were removed, and polished into a fine product that would serve some real practical purpose.

I don't know who owns the factory now, but it is poorly maintained and looks almost unused, at least from the Heath Road end, although there is a security sign – Imperial Security Services – so it must be occupied and operational. The rendered façade that I remember as pale green is now painted a pale chalky blue with a navy stripe. Ivy climbs over the side wall, penetrating cavities and roof spaces, and the cement slab in front is cracked with clumps of sprouting weeds. Dad would never have allowed such negligence.

A dilapidated fibro cottage to one side of the factory was occupied in the early 1950s by a family who briefly impacted our lives. The daughter was my arch-rival in athletics and the mother was Dad's bête noire, an interfering, complaining old biddy who made his first years in the factory rather difficult.

There used to be a greasy, noisy little office near the factory entrance where he insisted I work occasionally during mid-year school holidays – answering phones, placing orders, and filing invoices and receipts. I dreaded those occasional stints; he was a strict boss, and I worked under the constant stress of making mistakes. Years later, rather than face his constant criticisms for failing to invoice properly and cutting off valuable customers on the primitive switchboard, I preferred a mind-numbing job at Yates, counting flower seeds into tiny packets.

He always seemed at home in his grey boiler suit, supervising his young apprentices, teaching them to respect their machines. I daydreamed that he was a different kind of father: one who wore a tweed jacket with leather patches at the elbows and sat in a book-lined study sucking on aromatic pipe tobacco, or a poet with a fevered brow and haunted eyes.

I think that had he ever written then, he might have been an angry and mocking playwright somewhat in the mould of John Osborne, but he wasn't literary, and as a teenager, I really didn't appreciate his abilities or understand that creativity can take many forms. Dad epitomised the saying that 'necessity is the mother of invention', and in his own words he was always 'pregnant with possibilities'. His practical – rather than fanciful – inventions came to life in that little factory on Heath Road, and as his business expanded in the early 1950s, we moved to 38 Oberon Street.

It was a bigger house on a hill only a few kilometres from Terry Street, although it could have been a world away. The block of land was not large, but our backyard, like those of our neighbours, opened onto a small reserve that served as a private playground. The front of the house faced onto a large, sloping, bushy area with a lot of feathery casuarinas, stripling eucalypts, and tracks that led down to the shopping area from which I took the bus each day to school.

The house itself was made of apricot-coloured bricks, with a garage underneath and a wide tiled flight of steps – ten, if I remember correctly – leading to a patio built over the garage. Despite its modern form, our new home still had an outside toilet. Sometime later, Dad built an extension right along the back where he began showing Hollywood movies on his newly acquired projector, films that arrived in tin canisters and had to be picked up and deposited at the Hurstville railway station every few weeks.

On one of my weekly visits to the nursing home, I take a detour and wind up the hill to the house at the end of the cul-de-sac where I spent my adolescence. Unfortunately, I realise too late that it's often not a good idea to return to significant places from our past.

The house looks sad and rundown, its grounds unkempt. Several garbage bins, a plastic wheelbarrow, and dead palm fronds litter one side of the uncut front lawn; a rusting trailer is pulled up on the other side; the driveway is a maze of cracks; and there's a fold-up plastic clothes line on the patio.

The paling side fence needs fixing – the fence that once separated us from our wealthy 'Bible-bashing' neighbours who held evangelical meetings in a few Nissan huts built adjacent to their tennis court. They regarded Dad as a sinner because he drank alcohol and supported gambling by selling raffle tickets for charity.

'Just use your common sense when you go next door and listen to what those dills are telling you,' he said when I reported his sinner status. I remember asking him once if he thought there was a God. 'How the hell would I know?' he said. 'I think people just make up a God and a devil to suit themselves. I don't need some God to tell me how to do the right thing.'

He didn't believe in yoking children to a faith that would be difficult to cast off later. Maybe he hoped that if we were exposed to the bigoted beliefs of our neighbours, we would eventually make up our own minds about religion.

The only thing that has improved since we lived in Oberon Street between 1955 and 1961 is the bush regeneration in the reserve opposite, which is now protected and called the Church Street Native Flora Reserve.

*

There's an enlarged glossy black and white photo of our Oberon Street home as it was in 1957. Mum and I are out the front. She's in a flared flowery dress, I'm in my hockey gear, and we're standing in front of the open garage revealing the tail of a large Ford Fairlane station wagon: BEF 448. A metal swing lounge with yellow vinyl seats – made by Dad, of course – occupies most of the patio.

But my attention is not drawn to the figures, the car, or the swing lounge, but to the front double doors and the rooms beyond. That was where, two years before the photo was snapped, I suffered months of painful maths coaching, and where an incident occurred that defined my relationship with my father for years.

25

Not Quite Good Enough

Dad was standing behind me, leaning over my shoulder. His breath was warm on my neck, and there was a trace of his familiar smell: machine oil and Solvol soap for 'hard-working hands'. I sensed his grey-blue eyes boring into the top of my head and heard the ominous demand in his voice. 'Well?' He pulled out a chair and sat down. 'Come on, get that brain of yours working. How are you going to find the height of that building?' The fingers of his right hand drummed on the Formica tabletop; mine scratched away at the wooden underside, wishing it were his face.

An image of a right-angled triangle with its letters in upper and lower case swam on the page. The hands on the wall clock moved in slow motion, and the closed frosted glass sliding doors kept me imprisoned. My younger sister and brother were yelling in the backyard, and Mum was rattling around in the kitchen, banging a saucepan and opening and shutting the cutlery drawer. The warm beefy smell of casserole teased my nose and taste buds, and I willed the frosted doors to open, for her to call out, 'Time to set the table.'

'Say something, Pam – any bloody thing.'

I brought my right hand from under the table and flicked the pages of the second-hand book of trig tables. The symbols taunted me, and under my breath I recited the stupid mnemonic about Hitler he'd made me learn to remember the sine, cosine, and tangent ratios in a right-angled triangle. That was months before, when he'd taken me in hand, announcing that 60 per cent was just not good enough.

'Come on. Any idiot can do it!' My eyes prickled. He heard the sniff as I choked back the sob forming in the back of my throat. 'Don't bung on that act with me. Blubbering won't help improve your exam marks.'

'I just can't work it out, Dad. Please, can we stop now?'

He exhaled loudly, shoved his chair back, and strode to the sliding doors. 'Go and help your mother then.' His mouth was pulled tight at the corners. 'But don't think I'm giving up.'

The thudding in my chest eased somewhat. Maybe I'll be cleverer tomorrow.

*

Two weeks passed. I raced all the way uphill through the bush reserve from the bus stop and charged around the back of the house, hurdling my little brother's discarded scooter and tricycle. Breathless, I waved the report in front of Mum, who was at the kitchen sink in a freshly ironed floral afternoon dress. She dried her hands and studied the various marks and comments, and then propped the report against the oranges and bananas in the blue ceramic bowl sitting in the centre of the kitchen table.

'He'll be so pleased,' she said, giving my arm a squeeze. 'Now go and get changed, and come and help me peel the potatoes.'

His car pulled into the driveway. I was all fluttery inside. 'Bloody kid,' I heard as he moved my brother's toys from the side path.

'Darl, can you please make Peter put his things away when he's finished?' he said as he walked up behind Mum and planted a kiss on her cheek. 'Dinner smells good.'

He turned to me. 'How was maths today?'

'Okay.'

'Just okay?'

'It was good, Dad.'

He took a beer from the fridge and settled at the table with his newspaper. 'What's this then?' He'd seen it.

I didn't answer, waiting instead for the accolades: a smile, a 'well done', even perhaps a proud fatherly hug. But he simply gave the report a cursory glance, replaced my year's achievements against the fruit bowl, and returned to the evening news.

I looked at Mum for support. 'Just wait,' she mouthed.

Eventually he looked up. 'Pam, if you can get 98 per cent, you can get 100.'

*

From the perspective of almost half a century, it's hard to understand the persistence of that memory of the missing 2 per cent, when so much else about my life in Oberon Street seems to have been forgotten. And it's impossible to relive the intensity of the emotions I felt then. But what I remember happening is that I stormed off to my bedroom, sobbed for an hour or so, and remained in a sullen torpor for another few, focusing on a photo of the late James Dean as Jim Stark – full of sullen teenage angst – in *Rebel Without a Cause*.

Had I been a modern teen, I would have immediately got onto Facebook and let loose to my hundreds of friends and followers about what a dickhead my father was, and I would have discovered in turn all the other dickhead fathers or bitches of mothers out there.

But in those days, the only choice I had was to confront Dad – who would have simply said, 'Don't be such a bloody dill; get over it' – or smoulder in silence. I chose the latter and adopted a peeved expression that led to an edgy relationship with him. And I began seeing everything from the negative perspective of never being quite good enough.

Over the years, I would drag that incident out of the box of my subconscious like an important document to announce, 'See – that explains it. That's why I'm the way I am.' At unexpected moments, that hurt 13-year-old with a deep sense of injustice would emerge and gnaw at my self-esteem

I wonder now whether that story of the missing 2 per cent, told so many times over the years, bears any resemblance to the original experience. Could that one incident have really had such an effect? Or is my memory not of a single incident but a compilation of painful teenage experiences?

*

As with all teens, my emotions troughed and peaked like an ocean after a cyclone, but in late 1956, there was a brief lull when two significant developments in Australia shifted my focus briefly from myself to wider affairs: the British atomic testing at Maralinga in South Australia and the introduction of television.

I knew little of the Australian paranoia at the time – 'Reds under the bed' and Soviet spies operating in Canberra – but a newspaper photo of an ominous 11,400-metre-high radioactive mushroom cloud from Operation Buffalo–One Tree absolutely terrified me. I waited in dread for the fallout to drift across to Sydney, believing we were all doomed to die from acute radiation exposure. I prayed and promised to be a better person, kinder to my siblings, more helpful to Mum, and less sullen with Dad. And I was for a while.

It was about the same time when – in a crowd outside a local electronics store – I heard Bruce Gyngell in a TV test transmission say, 'Good evening, and welcome to television,' followed by Chuck Faulkner – with his American accent – reading the evening news for the first time. About eight weeks later, Dad bought one of the first flickering sets available on the market, and on 22 November, a large group of family and friends gathered in our home for the opening ceremony of the Olympic Games in Melbourne. Over the next fortnight, I was hypnotised by the gold medal performances of our swimmers and athletes.

Unfortunately, I also realised that due to my recent failure to win a place in the State athletics, I would never be good enough to be a 'Golden Girl' like the 18-year-old Betty Cuthbert. And it wasn't long before I returned to my default mode and began chronicling my miseries in a journal: every withering look from Dad, every ignored request, reprimand, and criticism. I seized upon them, studied them for hidden nuances, and added them to the list of things wrong with me.

*

Around the same time, during the Christmas holidays, I cut my reddish gold hair really short and dyed it what the sachet said was a rich auburn. But the colour was a disappointment; it wasn't rich auburn at all, it was more like a clown orange.

'You're not leaving the house looking like that,' Dad said. 'What the hell is the matter with you? Always wanting to change, never satisfied with who you are.'

Well, you're not satisfied with who I am are you? I thought, but brushed off his comment with, 'I'm a chameleon, Dad.'

'A bloody what?'

'The lizard that changes colour.'

'Well, if you want to change so much, then try following your mother's example. Look at her. Always just right. And go and get that muck off your eyes.' He turned to me again and said, 'Find something to cover your hair. You look ridiculous'.

Yes, of course: ugly and ridiculous.

Perhaps a year later, he exhorted me to take a leaf out of my mother's book. I didn't bother asking which leaf that was exactly, and it left me free to interpret it in any number of negative ways.

Looking back now, I can see that his comment probably had something to do with the fact that Mum was diplomatic, and I was a budding confrontationist. Maybe he hoped it would not become full-blown and could be toned down somewhat if I followed Mum's more feminine and tactful example. But if that was what he hoped, he must have been disappointed. My argumentative personality *did* develop. How could it not, when I was so much like him?

Years later, I read in Simone de Beauvoir's *The Woman Destroyed* that 'fathers never have exactly the daughters they want because they invent a notion of them that the daughters have to conform to'.

26

Rearing Its Ugly Head

It wasn't long before Dad was convinced that something undesirable, lying hidden within me, was about to 'rear its ugly head'. If that was *his* fear, it was not *my* reality. Of course I had fantasised about James Dean and Elvis Presley, but I was certainly not interested in the *real* thing with a teenage boy. I still preferred being with my girlfriends – who, like me, were natural competitors both inside and outside the classroom. All the same, just the possibility of sex rearing its ugly head meant someone had to give me a talk, and it turned out to be Dad.

I had menstruated at 11, earlier than most, and at the time Mum had given me a booklet called *What Every Girl Should Know*. Rather than being a book about an important rite of passage, it was basically a book about a hygiene crisis, with advice on how to keep clean and avoid smelling; how to attach sanitary napkins to a sanitary belt; and the need to avoid swimming and wearing white during menstruation. There was nothing about the actual process of sex, although there might have been some stick-figure illustrations of the missionary position.

In the 1950s, there were only indirect references to sex in magazines. People didn't discuss it in public, and the word *contraception* was banned from the radio. I guess I picked up what I knew the way most teenagers did when I was growing up: a few comments here and there within the family, and illicit and ill-informed conversations with school friends. That was, until Dad felt the need to have his talk.

Initially, he didn't give me the nitty-gritty of the actual sex act. His 'talk' was more to do with the need for abstention and retaining my virginity until marriage, as he and Mum had done apparently. I couldn't possibly know if what he told me was true, and I didn't question him about it, but I did react fiercely at the unfairness of 'It's always up to the girl to say no'.

'Why can't a boy take responsibility for his actions?' I asked.

'Well, of course boys have to. If a girl says no, then that's it, no question about it,' he said. 'But remember, any male will take it if it's handed to him on a platter.'

I suppose it's possible some nubile native girl in New Guinea offered 'it' to Dad on a platter when he was 20, but I doubt it, for he was fond of saying, 'If it's good for the girl, then it's good for the boy.' And Mum had obviously never handed 'it' over.

'It's the girl – and of course her family – who suffers the shame and humiliation of an unwanted pregnancy,' he added.

Was he thinking of his own mother's situation and the abandoned toddler, Robert, left behind in England – the child she never saw again? Or was it the shotgun marriage of his parents-in-law that he'd been told about and the ostracism they supposedly suffered for years at the hands of their families? Perhaps his concern stemmed from the moral panic that pervaded Australian society in the 1950s, fuelled by sensational press reports about the sexual license of bodgies who, like 'wolf packs on the prowl', threatened unsuspecting girls.

I have since discovered that magazines – like *Pix,* the *Post,* and *People* – frightened parents of the time not only about illegitimacy but also about the perils of petting and daughters becoming 'wild'. Blame for the latter was laid firmly at the 'primitive rhythmic beat' of rock and roll music, the 'frantic sex shows' of gyrating stars like Elvis Presley, and the brooding disaffected celebrities of the time who could corrupt even the most reserved of girls. Maybe it was because I listened to Elvis and Bill Haley on the Top 40 and had posters of a surly James Dean and fleshy-lipped Sal Mineo plastered on the back of my bedroom door that he was motivated to have his talk.

A few days after he initially broached the subject, I confronted him with something I *was* curious about: how people prevented unwanted pregnancies. Looking back, I'm amazed that he didn't seem embarrassed or say – as I imagine a lot of men might have – 'go and ask your mother'.

'Contraception, Pam.'

'But what exactly is that, though?'

'Well, there are condoms, of course. Some people call them *rubbers* because they're made out of latex. The man has to roll it onto his …' I raised my hand for him to stop. 'Yuck, that's so disgusting! Please, I don't want to hear any more.'

But he ignored me and continued. 'Then there's always "getting off at Redfern".' He smiled at my confusion and waited. 'Well, don't you want to know what that means?'

I was not sure I did; the whole sex thing sounded so difficult and ghastly. But on the other hand, it would give me an advantage over my friends and something scandalous to whisper about at recess or at the bus stop.

'All I know is that Redfern is that station just before Central. So if I got off the train at Redfern, it would probably mean that I hadn't quite reached the main part of the city.'

'Exactly,' he said. Satisfied that I had grasped the significance of the expression, he moved towards the door. 'Sometimes it's referred to in Latin as *coitus interruptus*,' he added. 'But that's enough for one day.' And off he went; he'd done his duty.

I was still confused, but he'd left me a clue, and I went searching in my Latin dictionary. *Coitus*. I said the word over and over then marked the page. *Interruptus* was pretty obvious. So 'getting off at Redfern' was breaking off intercourse.

I lay on my bed staring at the ceiling – something I did often in my teen years – mulling over this mystery. There were things I still did not understand. When would the man and woman know when to do this? Get off at Redfern, that is. Would they always be thinking of when to do it instead of being romantic? Could a man really stop himself? Where would the man's stuff go if he did? Wouldn't it be horribly messy? Could this method really prevent a pregnancy? It sounded a bit risky, because the woman had to rely on the man. Did they both enjoy sex this way?

I sat at my desk and made up a story to titillate my girlfriends, using everything Dad told me and what I had sussed out. Then I wrote a list of questions for us to secretly discuss behind the main building at school.

Over the next week, we couldn't wait for the bell to go off so we could resume our sex talks – but being romantics, I think we all finally decided that we would rather remain virgins than face the prospect of a rubber condom or the risk and mess of *coitus interruptus*. After all, we were only fourteen.

It is so difficult now to relate to the conservative, moralistic, and fear-filled 1950s: the terrifying prospect of an unplanned pregnancy, the shotgun marriage with its humiliation and ostracism, the heartbreak of forced adoption, or else a botched backyard abortion with the prospect of death. I wonder how many girls and women back then were tricked into believing that their partners would 'get off at Redfern', how many married women simply gave up having sex altogether, and how many husbands slept in another room.

Just imagine a world with no pill, and no magnum or size-to-fit condoms, no studs and ribs to stimulate the g-spot, no kaleidoscope of colours and fruity flavours. Just imagine the world of teenagers back in the 1950s when sex began to rear its ugly head.

27

A Bridge, a River, and a Lion

I have planned to take Dad down to the Georges River on my next visit, the place he once knew so well. I'll stop at one of the seafood outlets on the Blakehurst side of Tom Ugly's Bridge and then park in the reserve lying in the bridge's shadow, hoping it might trigger some reaction or a long-forgotten memory.

As we approach the bridge, I point to a driveway that once led to a famous local nightclub – Dora Skelsey's Ace of Clubs – and ask if he remembers it. He doesn't respond. 'What about the Waterfront Lounge?' I say. It was the name my parents' friends gave the old Skelsey nightclub when they transformed it into a fancy function centre with an attached motel.

'Silly old bugger burnt to death.'

For an instant I take my eye off the road to look for his reaction. I can't see his eyes, but his mouth is a firm line, his jaw tensed.

It's true. Harold, the owner, *was* killed in a fire that raced through the motel. I remember when it happened but have no memory of how that tragedy affected Dad at the time; he was a man who never spoke of his losses.

We reach the bridge, with its strange name. It was opened when my father was barely 12. Some believe it was called after Tom Iggley, a local fisherman; others say it was named after an Aborigine called Waggerly Tom who had only one leg.

From 1943, when my parents moved into the area, until they left the suburb over half a century later, Tom Ugly's Bridge and the area around it played a significant role in our family life. Dad sailed and motored under it and fished in its vicinity, and eventually we lived in a house that overlooked this unusual grey structure.

Halfway across the bridge, he stirs. 'This is a truss bridge.'

I'm not sure I've heard correctly. 'A what?'

'Six Pratt trusses.'

I glance at him quickly. His once practical hands lie unmoving in his lap. 'A truss bridge, eh?' I ask, trying to keep the conversation alive and wondering how he knew this. He was a mechanical, not a civil engineer.

I wait for him to find his way, but that's it. He resumes looking into the middle distance.

Although I should leave the silt of his mind undisturbed, I can't resist trying to dredge it again as I pull over past several blocks of luxury apartments on the site of the once famous Sea Breeze Hotel. I ask him if he remembers it. His face clears a little and then clouds over again. I mention the name of one of his wealthy Lions Club friends who once owned a waterfront restaurant opposite the Sea Breeze. But still no response.

Dad joined the Lions in 1953, and for much of the next thirty-four years, his life centred on the friends he made through that charity organisation. They were a unique breed of men who always had fun doing good deeds that made a difference to the lives of others. Many of our May school holidays were associated with their various activities and interests, including trips to interstate conventions that Dad used as opportunities to give us new experiences. He was always saying, 'This will be a new experience for you.'

*

'Right kids, we're off to Adelaide.'

Mum cleared the remains of tea, we gathered around, and he spread out a large coloured map of south-eastern Australia on the kitchen table. NSW was marked in pink, Victoria in yellow, and South Australia in orange, all covered in black spidery squiggles and dots: roads, railway lines, and country towns.

'This is the way we're going to drive,' he said. With a red pen, he started tracing from Sydney along a major highway until it reached Victoria, where he drew a circle. 'That's Wodonga and Albury on the Murray River,' he said. 'Then we're going to turn west and travel along the Murray Valley Highway to a place called Echuca and then on to Mildura.' Another two red circles. 'So Pam, what do you know about the Murray River?'

I told him; he was satisfied.

'And what about the Darling?'

He continued to bombard me with questions as he wielded his red marker and traced our upcoming trip into

South Australia: Renmark, the towns of the Barossa Valley, and Adelaide.

'Seems a long way by car,' Mum said. 'With the kids.'

'We need to see as much of Australia as possible,' he commented, excited.

'Where will we stay?' I asked

'Don't you worry about that. I'll get it all sorted.' He folded the map and put it away.

A month later, we were in a country hotel, I can't remember where or what it was called. It could have been the Royal, the Railway, the Commercial, the Exchange, or the Grand. The name doesn't matter. We were all dressed up for a six o'clock dinner in the pub's dining room. Unlike most of the bistros in country hotels today, the tables were set with white linen cloths and white linen serviettes, each folded in what Dad told us was the shape of a mitre. There was a small bread plate to our left with a gold rim, and a butter knife and six pieces of heavy silver cutlery. Just above the knives were several glasses.

'This is your first lesson in the right way to set a table,' he said. 'Take a careful look. It won't hurt you to know how it's done in hotels and how to use cutlery properly. When we get to Adelaide, there might be even more utensils on the table.'

He used his finger as a pointer. 'You start from the outside – say, the soup spoon – and move in with each course. That's the salad fork … ' And so it went. At each country hotel, we learnt something new. 'There's no excuse for bad behaviour in public places,' he was always telling us.

*

I pull up outside a dubious little shop smelling of heated oil and burnt onions. It sells fish and chips, hamburgers, and frozen bait. I'm tempted to go somewhere else, but the fish looks okay. I pass Dad the polystyrene containers while I do a U-turn further up the highway, drive down to Dover Reserve, and park facing the river with its faint mix of salt, mud, and diesel.

Between mouthfuls of greasy batter, I chat about this and that, but Dad fiddles with his food and says nothing. I give up and join him in his silence. Maybe he's having thoughts but just can't find the words.

There's not much movement on the river, just the occasional bow-wave of a passing craft and the slap and suck of the water against the slimy green rocks below. Squawking seagulls circle in the air above us waiting for the feast of leftovers, and like them, I circle, searching for memory scraps of the man sitting beside me and for my adolescence spent on and around the river.

Every year, the Kogarah Lions held what they loosely referred to as a Mardi Gras at this exact spot. Strings of coloured lights along the water's edge, their shimmering reflection competing with the lights from the bridge; rows of little tent-like booths spanning out from the sea wall creating dimly lit alleys where teens could steal a kiss or two; a temporary wooden dance floor – these images I can still see, but I have to imagine the *pop popping* of the shooting gallery; the clunk of the balls swallowed by the laughing clowns; the thump of the bumper cars; the sickly spun sugar smell of fairy floss; and the icy taste of snow cones.

I ask him if he remembers. He looks vague. 'No,' he says.

But I remember one such carnival. I was in my mid-teens, dressed in an aqua dress with shoestring straps and a flared skirt over a rope petticoat. I flirted with a handsome young bagpipe player in a Scottish band.

'You were always so busy in those days with your community work,' I say, but my words seem to wash over him. 'Like running the Lions' lucky-numbers wheel on the ramp at Hurstville station.'

If he is struggling to find an image, I have no trouble remembering, because it embarrassed me to see him there on a Saturday morning, dressed in his purple and gold silk Lions shirt, with a leather pouch around his waist where he kept the tickets and money. If I happened to be in Hurstville, I'd scurry past him, eyes averted as he joked with passers-by, urging them to get their lucky numbers before the next turn of the wheel.

I put my hand on his arm. 'Thanks, Dad,' I say. He turns and looks me straight in the eyes. 'For all the charity work you did as part of Lions,' I explain. He has no idea how little I cared about all the 'good works' stuff when I was an adolescent.

I unscrew the cap on a bottle of water, pour the liquid into an anodized mug, and exchange it for the polystyrene container on his lap. He takes a few sips.

'Would you like to stretch your legs?'

'No thanks.'

I dispose of the remains of our lunch – Dad's fish is largely untouched – and like a scene out of Alfred Hitchcock's movie *The Birds*, the seagulls swoop down on the garbage bin. As they begin their voracious screeching and squabbling, I snatch at a memory that floats across the water, a memory of a long-ago gathering of men and women on the veranda of a newly constructed building. They were all dressed up; it was the official opening of the Kogarah Lions' purpose-built Truby King Baby Clinic. Mum and Dad were there, celebrating another Lions achievement. The clinic's gone now of course, like so much else, victim to the Department of Main Roads.

There's an ache in my chest as I realise just what an admirable man my father was. But when I return, he's like an unhappy child. 'Can we go now?' he says.

28

A Bus Trip with Harriet

The grey light of early dawn filters through the bedroom's vertical blinds. I've been fidgeting, turning, scrunching the sheet, adjusting the pillows, and sighing since 3.15 a.m., initially awakened by a dream fragment: a large, crudely constructed model bridge made from paddle-pop sticks that wouldn't stand up properly and kept falling down.

Beside me, my husband snores, a low-frequency *huggggh-zzzz-hnggggh-zzzz* punctuated by a louder snort and a clicking thing. I nudge him; he grunts and turns over. I begrudge him his peace-filled sleep and want to shake him awake to discuss my dream. But what explanation could *he* possibly give? He's not into analysing things like dreams or working with his intuition.

I try drifting back to sleep, but thoughts flit like birds in and out of the shadows of the past: a young boy believing he'd been abandoned at 13 or 14 to fend for himself, a young girl at 13 and 14 yearning to be valued for who she thought she was.

It's warm already, and I push the sheet to the end of the bed with my feet. My husband stirs, pulls it back, and wraps himself up like a mummy. The early morning traffic has already started growling down Clarence and Market Streets, and from somewhere along the hall drifts the aroma of freshly brewed coffee – an early riser. I'm tempted to get up and make myself a cup, but I continue to lie there, eyes closed, trying to empty my mind. My reluctance to get out of bed has less to do with needing more sleep and more to do with coming to grips with the fact that it's Thursday again.

Later that morning, by eleven o'clock, I'm past the airport, powering along General Holmes Drive, my mind on my shaky teen relationship with Dad. To my left is Botany Bay, grey and choppy, a dangerous place to be out in a small boat when a strong wind comes up. I turn right at Ramsgate past the site of the once-infamous Ramsgate Baths where Dad – keen for us to develop a competitive spirit – enrolled my sister and me in the swimming club and ran along the side of the seawater pool urging us on to victory. The rest of the drive out to what is affectionately known as the Shire is a blur as I attempt to unravel some of the knots in our tangled relationship.

When I emerge from the car park into reception, the first person I see is little Harriet Smythe sitting in a chair near the administrator's office, and then John Gardner, pushing his wife Mary towards the rec room for lunch, his hands more claw-like than ever.

'Hello, Mary,' I say, touching her on the arm, hoping she can understand when I say, 'You've got a really good man here. Enjoy your lunch.'

I've never seen their son; maybe he comes on Saturdays. Maybe like many family members he can't face seeing his mother like that.

'Your Dad's not here, Pam.' It's Craig. 'He's out on a short excursion in the minibus. Ten of them. Having a picnic lunch. Should be back about one thirty.'

I wonder why Harriet wasn't included and ask Craig.

'She eats her lunch in her room alone. Poor love, she gets a bit agitated with lots of people around her.'

Something prompts me to ask if it would be all right if I took her outside for a while.

'That'd be really nice, Pam. Just go over and tell her who you are and ask if she wants to go on the bus.'

Harriet is wearing what would be called a vintage dress: somewhat like the fifties floral Mum had on in the picture of Oberon Street, but with long sleeves. She wears stockings and navy shoes with a small heel. The halo of hair framing her face is carefully combed, and as usual, a cracked leather handbag is looped over her left arm. She is focussing on her right thumb working in circles, tracing around the faded red and yellow flowers on the skirt of her dress. I wonder if it's a comfort thing.

I say her name gently. She looks up. Her once dark eyes, cloudy with age, stare at me blankly.

'Hello, I'm Pam,' I say and look directly into those eyes, just as Helen advised. The hand on her lap goes to her forehead, and I see the blue veins like knotted string in her wrist and imagine her heart beating like a bird in danger.

'Would you like to go on the bus today?' I ask, and her face lights up.

She extends her hand with its long crinkled fingers. As I take it, I'm careful not to press too hard. Her skin is cold despite the warmth of the day, and I remember Mum's blue-white fingers and how she suffered in the winter. Out in the garden, it's overcast, the sky a mouse grey. She lets go of my hand and totters towards the bus stop seat, placing her bag on the ground and arranging herself somewhat like a pianist. I follow and sit beside her; she moves in close, and I can feel the thinness of her body through her dress and smell her perfume: lavender with a whiff of vanilla. Maybe it's her soap or face powder. I pat her on the arm and take her hand in mine. She turns and gives a weak smile, and my heart is breaking.

'It will be here soon,' she says, just as she did the first time I met her.

'Where will we go today?'

'Town,' she says, but then she gets a bit excitable. 'Oh! Gloves and hat.'

'It's okay, you look beautiful exactly the way you are,' I say, hoping to calm her down and thinking of Mum's need to be complimented about her looks. Whether Harriet understands or not, it seems to work. She pats her hair with her left hand, makes no attempt to remove her right from my gentle hold, and settles down to wait.

I say nothing, and for the first time I am comfortable with the silence, although I don't know what happens next.

Craig pops his head around the corner, gives me the thumbs up, and disappears.

'Here it comes.' She shifts slightly but doesn't stand; I remain where I am.

'Oh, oh, must pay,' she says, bending towards her bag on the ground.

'Don't worry, I'll pay today.'

She eases back onto the seat, and we stay like that for the duration of our 'trip' into the city. I wonder where she's going in her mind. Perhaps she is meeting someone on the corner of the David Jones Elizabeth Street store, planning to have lunch in the lower ground-floor cafeteria or in the darkened St James coffee shop next door, just like Mum used to do.

Although she probably lived in the Shire all her life, I imagine her as a woman of mystery: never married, lots of lovers, no children, living a bohemian life in Kings Cross as a singer in a smoke-filled jazz club, friend of artists and writers. I disappear into the fictional bohemian story I've created until I hear, 'Home.' There, sitting beside me momentarily, holding my hand, is my mother.

I walk Harriet back inside, wait while she settles into her seat outside the administration office, and then go in search of Craig.

'Craig, I can't wait for Dad to get back. Can you please tell him I came? I have something important to do.'

'Sure thing. Great what you did with Harriet, by the way.'

'Not as difficult as I thought it would be.'

*

I turn in through the large iron gates of the entrance to the Woronora cemetery and crematorium for the first time in seven years, winding my way among the trees, gardens, and tombstones towards South Chapel, where I park the car.

Mum's ashes are somewhere in a rose garden nearby. I have a vague recollection, an image of her plaque and its position in the bed, but there are so many numbered rose gardens. Although I walk systematically, or so I think, I'm led in a meandering circuit through row after row of plaques, rose bushes, and gardenias. It's hard to read the inscriptions, as some plaques are relatively old and dulled by the weather. Others are newer, the brass shiny, reflecting the afternoon light, and I have to bend low to decipher the names.

But I have no luck and venture further afield.

What motivates people who make frequent pilgrimages to the site of their loved ones' ashes or bones, leaving little vases filled with plastic or occasionally fresh flowers? Do they talk to the departed? Do they think the dead can hear?

What has motivated me today after all these years?

Could it be something about Harriet, who has no family? Or is it my failure to have really grieved for my mother?

Eventually, I give up looking.

Shit! What kind of a daughter am I? I can't even find my own mother's final resting place.

29

One Day I'll Show Him

In the second half of the 1950s, life for me went on as usual, with Dad continuing to fire his occasional arrows of criticism. We were both working hard: he, down at his ever-expanding factory steadily filling the family coffers; me, doggedly studying to show him what I could achieve, continuing to seek his approval.

It was 1958, a turning point for both of us: my final year at school, and Mum and Dad's first overseas trip together. For months before their holiday, which was to coincide with my Trial Leaving Certificate, Dad was particularly chirpy, Mum less so. It was the first time she would be away from her children and her first time in the air. People didn't fly too much in those days.

Closeted away in my cubicle of a bedroom caught up in my studies, I didn't fully register the departure of my parents for the USA with a planeload of Australian Lions bound for the international convention in Chicago. And I showed little consternation when my grandmother, staying for five weeks to look after us, lightly knocked on my door to tell me that the chartered Pam Am Stratocruiser had to return to Sydney with engine trouble. Lions legend has it that the in-flight bar went dry, and they were forced to return to replenish it.

*

I remember lying on my bed staring at the ceiling – something I did frequently when I wasn't at my desk or pacing backwards and forwards from wall to wall. My hair was greasy and would remain that way until I had mastered chromosomes, gametes, and the difference between mitosis and meiosis. Only then did I reward myself with a shower, although I put the long grey woollen skirt and baggy jumper back on; they were the only clothes I felt comfortable studying in.

There was a light tap on my door. I knew it wasn't my sister or brother; they'd been warned. It was Nan to tell me that the plane had taken off again and to hand me a tray with a cup of tea and some freshly baked scones with jam and cream. She was spoiling me; I was something special. No one in the family had ever progressed this far educationally. And I played on it. Why wouldn't I?

'Thanks, Nan,' I said and she smiled sweetly.

The smell of her 4711 Eau de Cologne wafted into my room. It was probably sprayed liberally on the crocheted linen handkerchief tucked in at the wrist of her cardigan. In the next day or so, one of my aunts was bound to come over and do Nan's hair: a bluish rinse and then a set with the metal butterfly clips creating stiff waves that lasted for a week. Like my mother, she was never happy unless her hair looked good. She believed that if you 'look after your hair and your feet, the rest will take care of itself'. She was fussy about dolling herself up in the early afternoon and putting on fresh makeup to go to the shops. 'It's not good to be seen in public in your work clothes,' she always said.

'Is steak and kidney pie all right for tea, love?'

'That's fine, Nan,' I said, although I was hoping it might be her Depression meat loaf. Everybody in the family loved it. She'd been making it for decades, and Mum once said that she thought it played a large part in winning over her sons-in-law.

Whatever she cooked tasted good, however, and I knew I'd be fed like a prize heifer throughout my exam period, finishing with a sandwich and hot chocolate for supper every night around eight-thirty.

When she closed the door, I adjusted the spindle in the grey vinyl-covered record player to fit the adaptor for the new Everly Brothers 45, 'Bird Dog', and then flicked through the revision timetable I'd drawn up for myself: two hours to go through my annotated copy of *Hamlet*, followed by an hour checking my notes on *Pride and Prejudice*.

I often wondered why I could absorb most subjects pacing backwards and forwards across the three-metre space between the desk and the bed while listening to any type of background music, but not so the dreaded and incomprehensible maths. For that, I sat hunchbacked at my desk in complete silence. If only it hadn't been necessary for matriculation. It was the thing that worried me most about measuring up in the Leaving Certificate at the end of the year.

Mum and Dad arrived safely in Chicago, Illinois, for the five-day 41st Lions International Convention. And while I sang along to 'Volare', focusing on the French ancien régime and desert landscapes, Lions contingents from all over the world marched – banners and flags held high – down Michigan Avenue in their gaudy purple and gold silk shirts to the blare and thump of American school marching bands.

*

The Trial exam was held in the school hall. I revised up to the very moment of surrendering all my notes to the doorkeeper: a volunteer parent who acted with suspicion and authority. I wanted to ask her if she had ever been confronted with the stress of exams like this, but I knew the answer. My breakfast – 'you must have a hearty breakfast,' said Nan – was still heavy in my stomach, and from time to time it rose up to the back of my throat. Would I vomit all over the first English exam paper? Would I have a desperate need to pee when I was halfway through? But once the order to turn over our papers was given, my fears disappeared, and I wrote speedily for the next three hours, getting everything down before I forgot.

I felt reasonably confident, but under no circumstances would I admit it to my friends. So I just said, 'It was okay I guess,' and refrained from any post-mortem.

For two days all was well, but on the third, I was a quivering mess: it was maths. When I scanned the paper, there was nothing – absolutely nothing – I could do. My mouth was dry, and my cheeks were hot. I was going to fail. I just knew it. I thought of Dad in Chicago and wondered if he gave me a moment's thought. I put down my pen and rested my head on my hands. A sense of failure overwhelmed me. It was as if I had a ton of bricks resting on my shoulders.

One of the teacher supervisors hovered at my elbow. Did she think I was sneakily looking at formulae written on the inside of my wrists?

'Is there something wrong?'

'I feel sick,' I said 'May I go to the toilets?'

'Come, I'll go with you.'

My friends looked up at the scratching of my chair on the floorboards. They raised their eyebrows as I left; I lowered my head under the crushing humiliation and headed for the toilet block with the suspicious teacher in tow. As I splashed my face and drank from the bubblers, I heard my father's voice: *If you can get 98 per cent, you can get 100.* I *had* to show him.

'I'm okay now,' I said, although I wasn't, and hurried back to the hall desperate to make up the time I'd already lost.

I read through the paper again and saw one or two things that I hadn't noticed before. I started on those. My confidence increased, and I went back to the beginning. The solutions were coming faster. 'I can do it … I can do it,' I said over and over to myself. I was on the last page with twenty-five minutes to go, and by the time 'pens down' was called over the microphone, I was almost through the last question.

'What happened?' my friends wanted to know, clustering around me.

'I just blanked out, thought I was going to faint.'

'That was sooo hard,' someone admitted. The others agreed.

Was it? Did I eventually find it easy because I didn't realize the difficulty of the questions?

When I arrived home, there was a postcard and a newspaper photo of the Lions parade. I threw them on my desk, put 'All I Have to Do Is Dream' on the record player, and collapsed exhausted on my bed.

For the next week, I lived in chaos as I tackled the rest of the exams – all of them an anticlimax to the maths. Another postcard arrived and disappeared under the mountain of paper, folders, texts, two breakfast bowls encrusted with the dried remains of Vita Brits, and a stale half-eaten sandwich. Nan never ventured into my room without permission, and I showed little interest in the exciting periodic reports of everything my parents saw as they travelled beyond Chicago after the end of the convention.

When I eventually tidied up my room and rescued the American postcards from the rubble, I read the brief comments from Dad urging me to 'Never give up' and 'Just do your best'.

*

I never did become a star at maths, but my efforts eventually paid off with Dux of the School – which, according to the reference written by our tough spinster principal, Miss Edna M. Taylor, was due not to my brilliance but to my 'great strength of character'. It's strange that not only can't I remember what Dad said about my report but neither can I recall how he reacted when I matriculated with a Commonwealth Scholarship to Sydney University three months later.

Most of my school friends received girlie presents for passing the final exam, like Marilyn's tan soft 'real' leather bag. When I complained to Dad, he said, 'Don't worry,

I've bought you something.' All hope for a personal gift disappeared when we drove to his factory. It was a shiny new lathe. He saw my reaction and adopted his *don't bother grizzling about it* voice. 'If you want to go to university, that's the only way I can do it.'

It's rather amusing looking back at it now, but it wasn't at the time. I did get a leather bag like Marilyn's eventually, but only after harping at my mother for months. Three years later, my sister received a milling machine. I don't know what my brother received when his time came. Perhaps Dad didn't need any new machines by then.

30

A Seventeen-Year-Old Parrot

I think Dad was ambivalent about my going to university, wanting to know what the hell I was going to do with such impractical subjects as English, history, geography and psychology. We were like contenders in a boxing match as I defended the humanities and he denigrated them. It seemed he was waging a subversive war against me.

At university, I was not in the beautiful and privileged group of girls who spent their days trawling for a future husband in medicine, engineering, or law. Neither was I in the 'superior' clique of girls who saw themselves as avant-garde and joined the university dramatic society, playing minor roles in revues and working behind the scenes, as well as helping out in the office of *Honi Soit*, the student newspaper. Little did I know that, despite their literary brilliance, those girls only ever hovered on the edges of the burgeoning male intellectual counterculture that revolved around Clive James, the witty editor of *Honi Soit*.

The group of which I was a part – mostly state schoolgirls and relatively naïve – never took up smoking or tried drugs, and never missed lectures or swanned into them late, looking glamorous or bohemian daggy, daring the lecturer to reprimand us. We never requested extensions to essay deadlines. But I did become a Communist for a week, attended a Libertarian Society meeting once, and wore purple and green stockings until Dad objected, seeing them as a sign I was not taking my precious opportunity seriously enough.

We envied those more confident and flamboyant girls who saw themselves on the brink of something exciting, which was why, when we weren't deep in the bowels of the library stacks, we gathered in the cafeteria of Manning House – the Women's Union – to watch them hanging onto the words of the likes of Les Murray, Mungo McCallum, Bob Ellis, and Richard Walsh. Although we didn't drink then, we used to trail behind the girls who did when they gathered at the Forest Lodge pub off Parramatta Road. We were always on the edge of the circle looking in.

I was only seventeen and still too needy of my father's approval to really go off the rails, but like all of us, I was desperate to find my own identity. And as a way of doing that, I enthusiastically latched onto the idea that the fissure separating the human brain into two distinct cerebral hemispheres was the divide between Dad and me. My limited and uninformed knowledge was gained during one of the regular sessions sitting around Manning, listening to the circle of older students who spent most of their days drinking coffee and discussing an eclectic range of subjects from poetry, philosophy, and psychology to economics and politics.

'You're a left-brain person,' I told him. He gave me his *what kind of idiot are you* look and shook his head. 'You're logical, mathematical and precise,' I continued, 'a practical genius.'

'And so what are you?'

'I'm more right-brained.'

'What, so you're illogical, imprecise, and impractical?' he said with a *gotcha* smirk.

'I'm more of a feeling person, more imaginative. I see the big picture rather than the details,' I boasted.

'What a load of unadulterated rubbish.'

And of course – as I was later to discover – it was. Most people don't use one side of their brain exclusively.

Throughout that first year at university, Dad seemed to mock almost everything I said, and I guess much of it *was* mockable – if that's a word – since I simply parroted others and dished up opinions I'd never thought through or researched for myself. But why couldn't he have just said, 'Well, that's one way of looking at it, but maybe you could also consider such and such'? No, not him – just constant derision.

*

He was dispensing drinks to a few friends in the family room at the back of the house. Mum, who was proud of my outspokenness – something *she* never exhibited herself in public – had invited me to join them. At some point, the conversation veered towards politics, and in an attempt to appear smart, I said something along the lines that Arthur Calwell might make a good leader of the Labor opposition and have a chance of defeating the prime minister, Robert Menzies, at the next election.

I really didn't know much about politics then and certainly had no strong feelings one way or the other about Arthur Calwell. To me, he was just an ugly old man.

'He's a Communist,' said one of Dad's guests.

'That's totally wrong,' I interjected, making it sound really passionate. 'Calwell loathes Communists; he's a staunch Catholic. He refers to Australian Communists as human scum, morons, and industrial outlaws.'

Dad, of course, couldn't wait to puncture my ego. 'Stop big-noting yourself, Pam. You're always shooting your mouth off. What makes *you* such an authority? Not long at university, and you think you know everything.'

Looking back, I can see that Dad's objection was more than that I was 'big-noting myself'; it was that Arthur Calwell, a former trade union official and a Roman Catholic, epitomised much of what Dad hated.

Dad never employed a unionist in his factory then; his men didn't need to be union members because he was a very fair boss, paid them well over the award, gave them plenty of overtime, took them out for drinks every Friday after work, and cared for their families' welfare. He used to say he didn't want some troublemaking unionist coming in, getting the men all riled up, and telling him what he should do in *his* factory.

His aversion to Roman Catholics – surprising considering his Irish background – was purely personal, based on the treatment meted out by a hard-line priest to his Protestant best friend and the friend's Catholic girlfriend. The priest, apparently, bullied the couple mercilessly in an attempt to break up the relationship, threatened the girl's family if they supported the marriage, and refused to marry them in the church. Eventually, he relented and administered their vows in his rubbish-filled study among the remains of his lunch, with Dad the only witness.

This episode might not have been the only reason for his anti-Catholic views, but it's what he always told us.

Australia was deeply divided between Catholics and Protestants when I was growing up, each group living in a different world, both sides equally bigoted. School kids from Catholic and Protestant schools mocked each other. And the prejudice went so far as employment discrimination.

To turn the subject away from Arthur Calwell, unions, and Catholics, one of Dad's drinking mates asked what I was learning about in psychology. I told him about our recent lectures on the effects of toilet training on kids' psychological development. They seemed to focus on that in Psych 1 in 1959.

'I've never heard such crap,' said Dad. He laughed at his joke, and then he asked more seriously, 'Is that really the rubbish they're teaching you at university?'

He turned to his associates. 'I don't know why I'm wasting my money on a tertiary education for her.'

31

The House That Greg Built

It is probably futile, but I do it anyway because it's become a bit of a habit and I feel uncomfortable going out to the nursing home without anything for 'show and tell'. Of course I know all the 'do you remember' stuff is for my benefit; it's my desperate attempt to keep my father from disappearing. He watches as I set out two photos of the house he built at the start of the 1960s, and I wonder what the hell he's thinking

*

Our lives had changed yet again. Dad rushed into the Oberon Street house, twirled Mum around, danced a few lively steps, and said, 'I've found it! East-facing, steep, but just right.'

'How much is it?' Mum asked.

'Don't know. It's not for sale … yet.'

'Well, how …'

'Don't worry, we'll get it. I know what to do.'

When my father wanted something, he usually found a way of getting it despite any obstacles in the way, and that's what happened when he decided on the site at Baldface Point, that tapering piece of land surrounded on two sides by the Georges River.

The land that was not for sale turned out to be not one but two overgrown waterfront blocks with a wilderness-like reserve on one side and an old brick house on the other. I'm not sure how he managed to negotiate with the owners, who lived in the old house, or how he was able to convince them to sell both blocks for a good price. I suspect they might have inherited the property and were having trouble paying land tax, which had been reimposed in NSW in 1956 after having been abolished for fifty years. Maybe he agreed to pay what they owed, or at least part of it. I can't really say.

But in 1960 – a year that began with a heat wave killing thirteen people in Sydney – Dad at the age of forty-one obtained the land he coveted and began doing things on a large scale. He cleared away the rubbish hidden for decades under the vegetation, including a rusted motorbike with a claxon horn, and exposed large rocks and rock shelves that became features of the site. Most of the gums were left. Next, he employed an architect to design a house that would blend into the steep landscape and have views of the Georges River and the bay beyond from each room. The first of his construction projects was the steep, sweeping concrete driveway that bisected the two waterfront blocks longitudinally and allowed cars to drive right down to the water. The second – even before the house was started – was one of the earliest domestic in-ground cement swimming pools, excavated out of the fourth terrace.

*

Now, Dad stares at the exterior shot of the house on Stuart Street and drags it closer. I wait, listening to the intermittent ping of a leaking faucet, muffled voices in the distance, and the buzz of a blowfly struggling behind a gauze wire screen. The day is hot beyond the windows.

'There's no boat,' he says.

'Dad, this photo was taken long before you bought your first one.'

'There should be a boat out the front.'

He continues to stare as if, by concentrating, he can will the boat to appear.

*

The exterior of the house on the waterfront at 114 Stuart Street reflected the colours and textures of the bush: the lower half rendered in a leafy green, the upper level in stained timber, the flat roof completely covered with fragments of river pebbles, and glass everywhere else. There were no fences to be seen, just a vast sweep of land to the water, scattered eucalypts, a few palms near the beach, and a grove of banana trees below the pool. To me, the only thing that detracted from it was the swathe of concrete driveway. But as I've mentioned before, Dad was a concrete kind of guy. On the adjacent waterfront block, standing stark and alone, was – according to a real estate friend – the 'most expensive rotary clothesline in Sydney'.

The house's interior featured a vestibule in large ceramic tiles and a wall of a warm-coloured brick forming the backdrop to a staircase lit by clerestory windows and teak and opaque glass pendant lights. Each bedroom, with a different coloured door and feature wall – so 1960s – had its own balcony. The massive living–dining room downstairs had a flock-papered wall all along one side, and the furniture throughout was what today would be referred to as retro. Behind the stairs and running the width of the house was a room with a green door: the rumpus room and bar. The kitchen and laundry were filled with all the latest mod cons: a huge free-standing freezer, a dishwasher, a garbage gobbler, a massive clothes dryer, and later, one of the first microwaves. All of the downstairs rooms opened via glass sliding doors onto a huge wrap-around covered patio.

And so began our life in the 1960s – one marked by new technology, a more casual lifestyle, and for Mum and Dad, a future full of exciting possibilities. Almost from the start, the house became the focus of many Lions Club functions, and Mum found herself a dressmaker for the clothes she would need for her increasingly hectic social life. The photos from that time feature crowds of people: men in shorts and T-shirts, laughing and drinking; women casually floating around the patio in their long brilliantly colourful muumuus, and Dad always centre stage, holding a drink, wielding BBQ tools as he presided over the cooking of steaks and sausages, or with his arm around Mum and smiling broadly. Dad was now in his element – king of his castle.

*

The second photo I place in front of him is of a crowd of relatives and friends gathered around the bar in the rumpus room. This was Dad's domain.

The bar had blue-grey wall tiles, a sink and bar fridge, ceiling-high storage cupboards, and mirrored shelves that reflected images of a strange collection of glasses, mugs, and beer steins in both pewter and ceramic. There were bottles and decanters of all shapes and designs: a bell, a barometer, a ship's lantern, a clock, a leather book, and a vulgar little drink dispenser in the form of Friar Tuck in a barrel that delivered a stream of spirits through his penis. Shiny ice buckets and folded tea towels were stored on the shelves low down behind the bar, with most of the regularly used glasses carefully washed and polished.

The bar was the one place that my father was not happy to share with others. He was obsessive about the way his glasses were washed, particularly those for serving beer. 'If you don't wash them properly, they won't hold a head,' he'd say, and if ever he poured a beer and there was no decent head on it, he knew someone had been fiddling behind his bar. Despite these rules, he was very generous with his alcohol, knowing from experience that 'most of the bastards always turned up empty-handed'. His grog was kept under the cantilevered balcony and in a place we called the cave – a space cut out of the rock behind the rumpus room. The old fridges installed in both those places were always kept chock-a-block with all kinds of beers, champagne, white wine, mixers, and soft drinks. There were piled boxes of spirits, of course, and red wine kept on hand for those visitors who drank it. Dad was always topping up people's drinks. If guests indicated they'd had enough, he'd say, 'I'm not forcing it down your bloody throat.' To him, a full glass was a sign of his hospitality.

*

Dad looks intently at the photo of the bar and then jabs his finger at something I'd failed to notice hidden behind the crowd.

It's a poker machine, an old three-wheel 'one-armed bandit' that came into his possession due to an early association with Len Ainsworth of Aristocrat, who started making pokies in the early 1950s. Dad began manufacturing the gears that spun inside those earliest machines sometime after they were legalised in 1956. I suspect it was about 1961 when he acquired his own poker machine, made a steel stand to support it, and installed it beside the bar. Family and friends fed it with shilling pieces. I think he returned the money or gave it to charity. It disappeared around 1964. Maybe he removed it because it was illegal to have one in a private home, but more likely, it was because he was just over it by then.

'Can't beat them, made to lose,' Dad finally says, still staring at the photo, a comment he'd reiterated many times over the years.

I feel I've hit the jackpot with this photo, but then, to top it off, he adds with the hint of a smile, 'the walloper'.

I'm not sure if he's referring to his friend the detective sergeant at Kogarah Police Station or to his brother-in-law of the Kings Cross Vice Squad, both pictured sitting at the bar. He hated cops with the exception of these two.

But there's another of his good friends holding court at the bar, with his sleeked down steely hair and spivvy moustache, who Dad doesn't seem to have noticed. Dudley was quite the scholar and occasionally quoted from *Hamlet*. With a beer in one hand, he would turn to me at the bar and, in his best Polonius rendition, give me the same advice that the old Shakespearean windbag gave his son, Laertes: 'This above all: to thine own self be true and it must follow, as the night the day, thou canst not then be false to any man.'

It's a quote I always thought epitomised Dad.

32

Marriage and Swinging England

Thursdays are becoming a nightmare for me, and I wonder how people like John Gardner cope with visiting their loved ones every day.

I start getting jittery on Wednesday. What will I do with him? What can I talk about? I am just not good at this sort of thing; I can't just sit and say nothing. Others in the family seem to handle their visits with less angst, although I can't say how they really feel.

I'm hoping this time that a photo I removed from my white leather wedding album – showing him at forty-four all spruced up in a dinner suit, smiling at me enveloped in French ribbon lace – might stir something in him. It doesn't. But I have something else with me that will surely interest him.

It's the yellowing invoice listing all the expenses for my wedding reception at the Amory, once an upmarket function centre in leafy Ashfield. The catering for one hundred guests cost 36 shillings and 3 pence per person, plus 13 pounds 10 shillings for four wait attendants. Then there was the two-tier wedding cake with real flower cake top; wedding autograph book; Herbie Marks and his musicians; car hire; place cards; plus alcoholic and soft drinks – total £312/11/8. I have to laugh to myself when I see among the list of drinks fruit cup, dry sherry, Brandy Crusta, Hock, Sparkling Rhinegolde, and Pims – so early 1960s.

But like the photo, this elicits no response. His eyes and mind are somewhere else. It seems that Helen was right about old people not caring about all the things we think might entertain them.

*

During my early university years, marriage had been far from my mind; I'd wanted to be on the move rather than settling down, and had, by then, decided that I didn't want to conform to what a man wanted me to be. I fantasised about remaining single and independent, knowing I could achieve more if I did – but unfortunately, the early 1960s was still a time that celebrated domestic life, when an early marriage and leaving the parental home to set up an independent household was the transition to adulthood.

But it was more than that. There was definitely a terror of becoming one of those iconic spinsters, like the various headmistresses I'd experienced and women often featured in films and literature. Most of my friends at university also had a fear of spinsterhood, which we believed meant lifelong sexual abstinence. We never thought of those often-ridiculed women as being successful or sexually active, only as poor pathetic non-feminine creatures. It was rubbish of course, part of a twentieth-century myth.

And so I accepted the diamond engagement ring presented to me by my accountant boyfriend as my friends and I disembarked from the SS *Canberra* on our return from a working holiday in New Zealand to start our fourth year at university. Despite the new ideas of the 1960s about how modern families could live, I succumbed to the expectations from family and peers that I would make a commitment and build some kind of structure for the future. I didn't have the guts then to stand apart.

I suspect Dad knew from the beginning that my fiancé was not a risk-taker, had no entrepreneurial inclination, and lacked an assertive spirit. I can still hear his disdainful comment: 'He's a bloody company accountant. For God's sake, Pam, they're as bad as public servants.' All the same, he spared no expense for my wedding in May 1963, just as he had for my twenty-first birthday only three months before, an event quite different from his own coming of age in the Morobe jungle of New Guinea.

Over the years, I often wondered if I deliberately chose someone completely different from my father: a man who wouldn't criticise me, who'd accept me just the way I was even when I was outspoken, maybe even a man I could control. On the other hand, maybe I chose the man I thought I deserved.

*

Since Dad is not interested in talking, I ask if he'd like to go for a drive.

'Not really,' he says.

So what the hell can I do?

'Okay,' I say, 'let's go and find a shady spot outside.'

I take his arm with one hand and carry a jug of water in the other. The heat has quietened the birds, and there are no other residents around except for Harriet Smythe, who is wearing a large hat and sitting at the bus stop with one of the nurse's aides. Dad and I find a spot in a corner.

I realise I have no idea of Dad's daily routine and wonder what he'd be doing if I wasn't here.

'Do you know that lady over there?' I say.

'That's Kylie.' He smiles.

'No, Dad, the woman she's with.'

'No.'

'Her name is Harriet,' I tell him. He turns and looks at me as if I'm mad. 'Harriet Smythe,' I say, wondering if she had been one of those old maids I had once dreaded becoming. He continues staring at me as if I've just uttered something in an alien tongue.

The silence swells around us, and my mind drifts back forty years.

*

Life was too short to put aside youthful adventures for the sake of a secure domestic future, so after only two years of living in a boatshed on the water overlooking the Royal National Park, my husband and I delayed our plans to build a house in the Shire, sold everything we owned, and took off overseas for three years.

Just as the prime minister, Robert Menzies, announced his commitment of an infantry battalion to Vietnam, we boarded the *Galileo*, headed for Genoa and then Munich to pick up a Volkswagen Kombi camping van. I was about to get a taste of the freedom I'd always wanted, unlike all those young men destined to head off to war in South East Asia and a future filled with death, post-traumatic stress, and alienation.

Six months later, I sent news home that I was pregnant. I had inadvertently left my contraceptive pills in the Kombi van in Athens as we hopped about the Greek islands.

I don't know how Dad reacted, although he probably reiterated his earlier statement about wasting his bloody money giving me a tertiary education. Mum said all the right things, despite admitting to not really wanting to be a grandmother at forty-five.

As I was no longer working, we lived for long periods on baked beans and soup, and so reluctantly I wrote to ask Dad if he could lend us £300 to help with all the baby requirements. But as soon as I dropped the letter in the red pillar Royal Mail Post Box in Teddington High Street, I regretted it.

For weeks, I waited anxiously. Then it arrived, a blue aerogramme addressed in his distinctive hand. I sliced it open, and even before reading I knew what his answer would be. Towards the bottom of the page, following Mum's concerns about my health, was his refusal loud and clear: 'Pam, it's up to your bloke to look after you now. Besides, things are a bit tough here at the moment. If you can't afford it, you shouldn't have fallen pregnant. But I know you'll both cope.' The rest of the letter was filled with what was happening at the factory and the latest Lions Club functions.

There's no denying his refusal was fair enough considering everything he'd already done for me. And he'd always made it quite clear that once a girl was married, she was her husband's responsibility. But all the same, I was hurt and vowed never to ask for anything from him again.

While the 1ˢᵗ Australian Task Force set up a new Australian base at Nui Dat, I was living in the frenetic and constantly changing subculture that the satirical magazine *Private Eye* described as 'odd, shallow and egocentric'. Although I never labelled myself a 'mod', the me that wanted to be part of the London scene wandered around Carnaby Street in Soho, looking in the windows of the gear boutiques, longing to make a one-off purchase like a trendy Mary Quant yellow cap or flowery tie. Sometimes I'd stroll along the winding Portobello Road browsing in the market stalls for unusual second-hand clothes.

As I ballooned, the 1966 April editorial of *Time Magazine* declared: 'London has burst into bloom. It swings; it is the scene … a city pulsating with half a dozen separate veins of excitement.' I sent the cover of *Time* and the editorial with a letter home, telling everyone about 'Swinging London' as if I were really part of it instead of sitting in my cold bedsit filling the gas heater with shillings and living vicariously through the actions of others as I had at university a few years before.

And speaking of shillings, while I was scrounging around for them at the bottom of various handbags to provide me with heat in the cold and gloom of a February London, back home decimal currency was introduced, and the shilling was replaced by a ten-cent coin. There were also anti-conscription protests, a strike by two hundred Aborigines employed on the Wave Hill cattle station for a wage of fifty dollars, and the election of the first ethnic Chinese mayor in Darwin.

The son I gave birth to around the middle of that year would be growing up in a completely different world than the one I had experienced.

33

Fishermen and Grandfathers

I've decided to take Dad somewhere near the water again, hoping it might have a soothing effect on him and allow me to feel more like a caring daughter.

The sign in and sign out columns in the visitors' book record how few hours a week I actually spend with him, though why I care I'm not sure, as I've seen more of him in the last few months than I have in recent years. In my place, Dad would have simply said 'stuff it' and left the book blank.

I drive the short distance from the nursing home to the dark green Woronora River lined with mangroves, casuarinas, picnic areas, and boat sheds. The hidden riverside village of my youth with its holiday shacks now features upmarket waterfront properties with jetties, although it still retains its sleepy refuge-like aspect, surrounded as it is by cliffs and native bushland.

We pull up near a walkway that follows the river for a short distance, and I help Dad to a bench a few metres from the water. His gaze immediately follows a number of brightly coloured kayaks barely making a ripple and a small tinny slowly putt-putting up the river. He appears a little confused.

'Is this the river?' he asks, meaning – I assume – the Georges River on which he lived for over three decades.

'No, Dad, this is the Woronora River. It's a tributary of the Georges.'

'Oh,' he says and, just as he did when I took him to Tumbulgum on the Tweed River Up North, continues to stare at the water. The kayak fishermen have taken up a spot on the other side among the mangroves, but I think Dad is watching the pelicans. There are two of them gliding in front of us, creating small v-shaped wakes.

I remove a can of beer and two small plastic cups from my bag, pour a small amount into one, and hand it to him. He takes a few sips, and I tip some into another for myself.

A middle-aged bloke with a hat tied under his chin – protective though horribly unattractive – sets himself up about 5 metres away. He opens up a stool and lays out lumps of bread and something else I can't identify on a hessian bag. Then he baits his rod with bread, casts off, and leaves the rod balancing against the wall as he begins hurling the stuff on the hessian bag into the river.

'Berley,' Dad says without taking his eyes off the fisherman, who then settles on his stool and waits.

The sun is warm, and there's not much noise except for the chatter of a child. An old man, probably her grandfather, holds her hand as they watch the pelicans, and I hear snatches of the Ogden Nash poem: 'A wonderful bird is the pelican, His bill will hold more than his belican. He can take in his beak, Food enough for a week, But I'm damned if I see how the helican.'

'Say it again, Poppy!' says the delighted child.

Against the child's laughter and the cooee call of a teen alerting a man on a heavy-duty inflatable boat, I hear – pushing through the fog of memory – little boys yelling at the tops of their voices from the Stuart Street patio.

My sons had just seen their grandfather in grey overalls emerge from below deck of the cruiser moored out the front. He waved to them, secured the boat, and rowed back in his little tinny. They rushed down the hill, hoping he'd relent and let them row out alone into the river, but they were still too young and not responsible enough, he told them, although he had at times let them sit at the wheel of the cruiser.

'Wooh there.' The fisherman lunges for his rod, its reel buzzing as the line plays out.

'Looks like a decent-sized one,' says the grandfather, and the fisherman lifts his rod, I guess to gauge the weight of the fish.

Dad spills his beer as he struggles to his feet and then shambles a few metres to be closer to the action. When the fish breaks the surface, he says, 'A bream, a silver bream.' I silently congratulate myself on having brought him down to the river.

'Yeh,' says the fisherman, 'probably about 30 centimetres.'

But the little girl appears distressed as he reels it in 'Throw him back, please man,' she pleads. Reluctantly, the fisherman unhooks the line and returns his catch to the water.

Dad looks as if he doesn't understand. 'Would've made a good meal,' he says.

In my mind's eye I see him in any number of photos, usually bare-chested, holding up his catch of the day. He may not have been a grandfather who took his grandchildren for walks and recited poetry to them, but he did show them how to gut, scale, and fillet a fish.

The old man takes his granddaughter's hand and continues on his way. 'Is there anywhere to get food down here ... a café or restaurant?' I ask the fisherman.

'There's the RSL further up on the other side,' he says. 'Or you might be able to get something at the Boatshed ... the Star Boatshed on Forbes Creek just past the RSL.'

I thank him, lead Dad back to the car, drive across the low bridge to the Sutherland side of the river, and wind my way through bushland past the RSL in search of the Boatshed.

An old timber two-storey building with what looks like a fresh coat of blue and white paint sits on the edge of a creek leading into the river. Brightly coloured kayak shells lie on their sides out the front; others are stacked on racks inside. Dad seems interested in the tackle and boating paraphernalia on sale.

'I was told I might be able to get some food here,' I say to a friendly-faced woman.

'Well, we're not really a food outlet, but I can make coffee or tea, and there are soft drinks, some homemade cakes or scones. And ice creams in that fridge over there.'

Dad is staring out at the water. 'That's fine, thanks,' I say, and she leads us out to a smallish blue metal table under an umbrella. I order coffee for Dad, tea for me, some juice, and a slice of custard tart and scones with jam and cream to share.

It's a beautiful day to be outside. Dad looks reasonably relaxed, and I'm feeling contented. A raft of ducks paddles across Forbes Creek, maybe hoping for some tasty titbits from our table. He's watching them, and I wish I could get inside his head.

The presence of the old grandfather on the other side of the river has triggered a network of memories of Dad as a grandfather. He was only forty-seven when his first grandson was born, a young man at the peak of his life. I watch him watching the ducks and an ibis that has wandered along the shoreline, and it's hard to recognise that young tough man in the slowly diminishing person in front of me.

He was a no-nonsense grandfather who wouldn't tolerate rudeness or lack of manners – particularly with the boys. But they weren't always aware of his signals and often went too far in fooling around: skateboarding down the steep Stuart Street concrete driveway, dive-bombing in the swimming pool, and of course racketing around in the rumpus room.

I can see them still. It must have been the late 1970s. They twisted and spun on the new orange bar stools with five-spoke chrome bases and ringed footrests, and on the black leather lounge chairs on their swivel metal bases. They flopped on the plump beanbags, making farting sounds. They dropped crumbs from Adora Cream Wafers and Sara Lee chocolate cake, the plates constantly replenished by Mum. They ran their fingers up and down the large cylindrical orange-red lava lamps. They sprawled on the floor waiting for the hard lump of wax 'lava' at the bottom of the large glass container to expand, become less dense than the coloured liquid, and slowly rise to the top. They rolled around the floor in hysterics at the bizarre shapes: long obscene shimmying columns and various sized globules that reminded them of interesting parts of the human body.

'If you don't shut up and stop flopping in the beanbags and swivelling on those stools, I'll turf the lot of you out,' Dad yelled. 'And keep your bloody hands off those lamps.'

I guess my father would have been impressed that Edward Craven-Walker got the idea for the lava lamp – originally called Astro – in 1963 while watching an egg timer made out of a cocktail shaker filled with liquids bubbling on a stove in an English pub. But I'm sure he would have been far less impressed to know that the lava lamp that so intrigued his grandchildren was an icon of the supposed Age of Aquarius, its constantly changing coloured display reminiscent of the psychedelic hallucinations of mind-altering drugs such as LSD.

'Do you remember the rumpus room lava lamps?' I ask – and then immediately wish I hadn't broken the silence by asking a question without any context. It's bound to confuse him. He continues chewing a morsel of scone, having already eaten the custard tart minus the crust. Then he smiles. 'Italy, with my girl,' he says.

Another one of his better days.

Perhaps it was purchases like lava lamps that help explain the few light-hearted words on several postcards he sent to my brother from Europe in 1972. 'Pete please see that there is food and grog available for us as we have no money left. No dollars.' 'Hope we have made a quid (Do we need it?)' 'Trip wonderful. But can't really afford it.'

'Dad, would you like an ice cream?' I ask, worried that he hasn't really eaten much. Surprisingly, he nods.

I wait until he finishes his little tub of slowly melting ice cream before helping him back to the car.

It's been really nice ... for both of us, I hope. When, on our return, I check the nursing home clock above the visitor's book, I am pleasantly surprised at just how much time we have spent together.

34

Alcohol and Family Brawls

For weeks, I've been digging ever deeper into the archives of my subconscious trying to catch onto anything that might give me a greater insight into my father and our relationship during the decades of the 1970s, 1980s, and 1990s. But I have to admit to knowing only the smallest part of what there was to know about him during that time. I moved further and further to the edge of his life as my own on the far north shore of Sydney swelled with the distractions of three sons and a full-time teaching career.

Had someone asked me back then what life in Stuart Street was like, I would have casually said, 'A vast, non-stop blur of good times: of money, boats, overseas travel, champagne breakfasts, progressive dinners, charity art shows, fashion parades, and Christmas picnics for disadvantaged children.' But if I were to search through the endless boxes of coloured photos from those years, it would seem that life was centred around boozy family celebrations and gatherings that involved a growing brood of grandchildren.

Although both of these views were to a certain extent true, they were simply high points in what would have otherwise been a relatively routine life marked by hard work and periodic financial worries.

In the early 1970s, while I was developing an interest in the feminist movement initiated by Germaine Greer's *The Female Eunuch*, Dad was more concerned with the effect of a worldwide recession on Australian manufacturing. His engineering business suffered badly, and Mum at fifty-three had to go back to work as his receptionist at the factory, her first time in employment in over thirty years. I can't say the nature of the financial stresses they faced, the degree of their debts, or how long their problems lasted, but Dad was not one to dwell on setbacks or to just wait for things to improve. He was proactive, always out and about soliciting for new customers and looking for fresh opportunities to keep his men employed and the factory operational.

Often, late at night, he would arrive home with prospective business associates and get Mum out of bed, still reasonably presentable in her navy velour tracksuit. Her job was to be the hostess, providing food – like smoked oysters on water crackers, corned beef sandwiches, cheese and bacon melt fingers, and large pickled onions – to soak up the alcohol as their business transactions went on long into the night.

There is no doubt that over the following decades, during both good and bad times, a large amount of alcohol was consumed in the rumpus room at 114 Stuart Street, which often lived up to its name as it erupted into sporadic disturbances or brawls. I have often wondered why it is that alcohol affects people differently. Is it something in our genes, some chemical make-up in our bodies, a behaviour we learn, or the result of life's experiences?

Mum was one of the quietly glazed, slurry drinkers, never causing any problems. I couldn't count the times I saw her balanced precariously on a bar stool, her legs elegantly crossed at the knees, still aware of the way she presented herself, smiling at no one in particular, thinking her slurred comments through pursed mouth were adding something of significance to the conversation.

Dad, on the other hand, moved through a funny loud phase and then, without warning, could flip and launch into verbal abuse. Like him, I was never quietly inebriated but outspoken from the beginning, and if my ideas or passions were challenged or ridiculed, I could become like Dad – verbally abusive. Other members of the family became positively maudlin.

*

As I search for incidents that reflect my later relationship with Dad, I am more convinced than ever of the accuracy of Virginia Wolfe's comment in *Moments of Being* that most of our memories of everyday life are 'nondescript cotton wool'. However, there are 'exceptional moments – those emotionally charged – that fly out at us loud and clear across the years'. Lying just below the surface of my mind are two such incidents.

The first occurred after my brother's wedding.

Dad was behind the rumpus room bar, of course, in a charcoal grey suit but minus his tie, pouring himself another Scotch. Mum, dressed in dusky pink, was carefully balanced on a bar stool, sipping a Scotch and water. My husband, seated next to her, dressed in a new brown striped suit, crème silk shirt, and Pierre Cardin tie, was drinking a beer; he appeared to be relatively sober. I was next, in a long red dress, gulping a white wine.

I have no idea what triggered the outburst, but like all those years ago when I was at university, Dad cast out the lure and waited for that moment when he knew I would become overemotional and take the bait. Unlike my mother and husband, I never tiptoed around conflict or skulked at its edges. No, I charged right in and vehemently expressed my opinions. I did it again, and as usual, he began to goad me, to pour scorn on my opinion, to laugh.

I turned to my husband, who said nothing. I looked at Mum, who said nothing. And at that moment, I despised them both. I went on the attack. 'For God's sake, Ken, why the hell don't you support me? You know you agree with me.' And I knew he did.

He squirmed and said, 'Just calm down.'

I was unable to control the rage building up in me. 'Just calm down?' Then louder, 'Just calm down? You are so fucking weak. You and Mum always sit on the fence, never commit to any opinion.'

'Don't *ever* let me hear you speak about your mother like that,' said Dad, his face reddening.

'It's okay, Greg,' Mum said, putting in something at last.

'No, it's not bloody okay.'

'Of course it isn't, Dad, can't upset Mum, she's perfect.' I clenched my hand holding the wine glass, wanting to smash it in his face.

'You can piss off out of here right now.'

I raised my glass as if in a toast, then turned and hurled the wine at my husband, the lesser of the two targets. Dad smirked, keen to see if he had any balls. Dripping Riesling, Ken got off his stool and deliberately and slowly poured his beer over my head. A whoop of delight came from behind the bar. 'At last!' There was iron in his laughter. 'At last you got the bitch! I always told you she was a bitch.'

The following morning, when I came downstairs, sick in the stomach with remorse at my bad behaviour – of course it had to have been my fault – I apologised to Mum but ignored my husband. Dad, cheery as ever, cooked a BBQ breakfast as if nothing had happened. 'Want fried tomato and onions with your eggs and bacon, darl?' he asked me.

Did he not remember the 'bitch' comment? I don't know; I never raised it with him. Maybe I was afraid to find out some unpalatable truth that might snowball into something else. At the time, I ate my cooked breakfast and rationalized the incident as simply a drunken outburst on both his and my part. It was certainly not the only one over the years.

But I suspect that for some people, alcohol induces a cruel honesty that cuts through the hypocrisy and diplomacy we live with day to day, and that what we say when our inhibitions are removed is what we really feel.

So if that is the case, and Dad called me a bitch when he was drunk, was that something he really thought at the time? And if so, why?

Perhaps he recognized something of himself in me that he didn't like, something that he thought inappropriate in a woman. Maybe he thought I was too outspoken, so different from Mum, or that I dominated my husband. Maybe it was my feminist stand on many issues. I'll never know, but for a while I incorporated the *bitch* label into my psyche – as I had done with other comments of his in the past – and let the poison fester.

It's hard now to analyse something that occurred so long ago, but I have to admit even now to exhibiting some bitchiness – usually triggered by too much alcohol – that manifests as scathing criticisms and wounding comments. There is certainly no excuse, but I suspect I still have a hurt adolescent at my core. It is possible that Dad did too.

The second incident occurred when my brother-in-law, celebrating his son's twenty-first birthday at Stuart Street, unadvisedly invaded Dad's domain behind the bar, replacing him temporarily as the host. We all should have known better, of course. The party atmosphere changed as if a storm front was moving in.

Dad disappeared to the lounge room where his anger – undoubtedly sparked off by alcohol – grew like a cumulonimbus cloud. When my sister and then my brother-in-law attempted to cajole him back to the rumpus room, he told them to piss off. Hoping I might have more luck convincing him to return to his rightful place behind the bar, I went out to him. 'Dad, you can't just sit here. Come back out and join in the celebrations.'

'Leave me be,' he said, his voice hard, his mouth clenched. He was not one to respond to wheedling.

'Come on, it's not fair on everyone.'

That did it! The full ferocity of the storm hit. He came at me, put his hands around my neck, and shook. 'Get out!' For the briefest moment, his eyes revealed a cold fury, and just as I thought he might choke me – well, maybe that's a bit of an exaggeration – his hands slackened, his eyes went blank, and he shook his head as if to clear it of some demon. He gave me a weak shove and disappeared upstairs.

Shaking, I returned to the family gathered in the rumpus room, unable to understand his fierce physical reaction to me. Mum, as usual, tried to smooth things over. 'Don't worry about him, I'll deal with him later,' she said, still in a partying mood. 'We haven't had the food yet.' But the festivities deflated like a leaking airbed.

If it was so important for Dad to be in control in his own home, why didn't he just say something to my brother-in-law when he first went behind the bar? Or was it really Mum he was angry with? Maybe he felt she betrayed him by remaining in the rumpus room enjoying herself while someone replaced him as the host. And just as I had poured wine over my husband all those years before, maybe I was the easier target for him on that occasion. Of course, I was not the only one in the family who occasionally felt his irrational anger.

There is no strong feeling attached to that scene when I relive it now, and I suspect it really had nothing to do with me. But I've often wondered why no one, except for Mum in private, ever confronted him about his periodically unacceptable behaviour, as they always did with me, and if over the years he ever laid a hand on his girl in an angry alcoholic daze.

35

Christmas: A Whole Load of Humbug

Christmas approaches: a time of celebration for some and of manufactured cheerfulness, family tensions, loneliness, and despair for others.

Mary Gardner, whose stroke had forced her into a living death, dies just a week before Christmas. A good thing for her, I'd say, although I don't know how it impacts John; I never see him again. I hope his wealthy and very busy son Tony will now take some responsibility for his father.

For the last seven years, despite Christmas invitations to come south and celebrate with family and friends, Dad either had to be prised out of Murwillumbah or chose to spend the holidays alone. Did he think we would see him as a nuisance, a bit of an extra now there was no Mum around? Or was his statement that 'Christmas is a whole load of humbug' how he really felt?

Although it was his choice, a stone of remorse for those years he was left alone Up North is lodged deep within me. But Dad is Down South now, and the family feels obliged to organize something, although there's a sense of reluctance in the communiqués that pass backwards and forwards between us. 'I suppose he can come to our place.' 'We'll have him if someone can bring him down.' But I think we all know he won't want to be organised and fussed over by us, and I suspect there is a collective sigh of relief when he declines our various offers and half-hearted appeals, choosing to stay at the nursing home.

So it is left up to us to make our own arrangements to see him, the man who for decades was the sun around which our family and others orbited each Christmas. Time loops back … to the Christmas party for disadvantaged kids held at Stuart Street every year; to grassy terraces pocked with fold-out camp tables and chairs, travel blankets, multicoloured umbrellas, and slowly emptying eskies; to young women in the latest bikinis giggling as they burned and older women in long dresses, floppy hats, and large tinted octagonal sunglasses posing and gossiping. Bare-chested men roared with alcohol-induced camaraderie, boisterous teens bombed and dunked each other in the pool, and little kids squealed each time they circled on the tinkling carousel. And then there was Mum, with a glass in her hand, weaving her way between the various groups, and Dad parading on his ride-on mower with Santa Claus calling out *ho ho ho* as he distributed presents to the kids.

As it turns out, the nursing home staff organizes a big Christmas function in a hall in a neighbouring suburb for all residents well enough to be transported by bus, and for any relatives who wish to join them. It's probably better for Dad than all the cajoling and carry-on of his extended family at someone's place far from the nursing home. I think of little Harriet, though, with no choices: no family and, due to her anxiety in large groups, no Christmas lunch with other residents. But will she even know it's that time of year?

Personally, I think we expect too much of Christmas.

*

It's stinking hot, at least five degrees above normal; the car's air conditioner isn't working; and we can't find the venue. My husband and I, having opted to join Dad at the nursing home celebration, drive around in circles, unfamiliar with this suburb. It's one of my second husband's rare midweek days off from the hotel. It's taken us forty-five minutes to cross the city and another forty trying to locate the hall. Tempers flare.

'Okay, I know. It's *my* fault.'

'I didn't say that.'

'I should have come alone.'

'I offered to come.'

'Well, stop being so picky.'

We pull over and I get out. The air sizzles and the blood pounds in my ears as I ring the nursing home to get more specific directions. By the time we locate the venue, it's too late; the hall is filled to capacity, and lunch is already underway.

Heat slinks around the entrance and sweat pours down between my breasts and thighs as we stand at the door like lost children scanning the crowd. Then I see him. He's jammed in towards the middle of the room wearing an orange paper hat.

'Why don't you go in so he knows we came?' says my husband.

'What about you?'

'No, I'll wait out here.'

Yes of course you will, and have a bloody cigarette, I suppose.

A largish woman with a dry voice asks if she can help me. 'We were supposed to join my father for lunch,' I tell her, 'but we had difficulty finding the place.'

She removes a handkerchief from her pocket and wipes away the glaze of sweat from her forehead. 'There's no spare room, I'm afraid; more relatives than we expected turned up. But we could set up a table for you here and organise some Christmas pudding, since you missed the turkey.'

Sure, just what I want: stodgy pudding covered in packet custard, in this heat.

'That's kind of you, thanks,' I say, 'but I just need to let Dad know we made it.'

I make my way down the side of the hall past a line of walking frames parked like supermarket trolleys and try imagining the chaos when the staff had to disconnect the patients from their safety support and negotiate them into the crammed area between the tables. In the overheated hall, there's an unpleasant cocktail of smells – old age, cooked meat, and something syrupy – as well as a medley of sounds – agitated animals in a zoo, the excitement of toddlers at a party, and *The First Noël* scratching away in the background.

When I reach the head of Dad's table, I stop, hoping he'll turn and see me, but the woman beside him – her head like a nodding parrot – seems to have captured his attention, although I don't know how he can possibly hear her over the general cacophony. Perhaps he's not even listening to her.

I've got to get to him, make contact.

I squeeze sideways along the narrow space between adjacent tables laid with festive plastic cloths and strewn with party hats, torn red and gold bonbon crackers, and discarded tokens. Scattered at intervals are jugs of cordial and coloured plastic mugs, and in front of most of the elderly are the remains of the barely touched Christmas roast – far too much food for ageing gastrointestinal systems.

There's a sense of Death waiting patiently for the festivities to end, already tugging gently on some of those in the room.

When I'm directly behind him, I touch him gently on the shoulder. 'Dad.'

He half turns. His face is flushed, his nose glowing with purple tracery. There's the hint of a smile. Or maybe not, for he says, 'What are *you* doing here?'

'Don't you remember? We were coming to join you for lunch.'

'Were you?' He doesn't ask where my husband is.

'But we got lost. I'm so sorry. Anyway, you look as if you're enjoying your Christmas party.'

'You call *this* a party?'

I suspect the only thing Dad would have called a *real* party was something *he* organised and controlled. I feel in my bag for the large squishy Christmas present wrapped in gold metallic-like paper. But if I give it to him now, it's bound to be left behind and end up in a garbage bin along with all the other Christmas trash at the end of lunch. Not that Dad would probably care. He was always a bit indifferent to presents, never one to respond enthusiastically to a gift unless it was something we had laboured over and produced ourselves – like the eight photographic albums I spent weeks making up for his sixtieth birthday and the framed collage, drawings, and cartoons created by my family for his seventieth. Generally, he preferred to be the one doing the giving.

'Merry Christmas,' I say, leaning down to kiss him on the forehead and give his shoulder a squeeze. 'I'll leave your present at the nursing home.'

There's no reciprocal Christmas wish, no expression of interest in the family, no attempt at further conversation. He turns back to the woman with the nodding parrot head. Am I dismissed?

Plates of Christmas pudding appear, and the scrape of a piano stool and a high-pitched whine announce the start of the entertainment. There really is no point hanging around.

'Well, I'll see you next week then,' I say and give him one last hug.

I hold back the tears at the thought that this could be his final Christmas. What if my last Christmas image of him is a half-turned head wearing an orange paper hat?

I escape from one hideous environment to another – the oven of the car park – with the pounding of blood still in my ears. God, I could have a stroke on my detour to the nursing home.

*

I leave my husband in the air-conditioned reception, tap in the security number for South Wing, find the casual nurse on duty, and hand over the present. She accepts it without

227

much enthusiasm. My husband's gone when I return, probably dragging on a fag, but Harriet is there alone in her usual seat, bird legs crossed elegantly at the ankles and a shaft of sunlight shining through her feathery hair. She has a silk scarf pulled tightly around her body and a straw hat balanced on her lap, one bony hand holding it in place.

I weep inwardly at her isolation from the others.

'Hello, Harriet,' I say.

She pulls herself up, places her hat at an awkward angle on her head, and takes my hand. Oh no, not the bus. But it *is* Christmas, so I ask her if she'd like to visit the city to see the Christmas decorations.

'Presents,' she whispers.

'Okay,' and we walk slowly to the bus stop. But the sun is beating down on its wooden seat and metal frame, and I have no hat. We won't be able to stay long.

While she travels to her favourite shops, my temples throb, and I become liquid. I wait as long as I can, and then I stroke her hand softly. 'Harriet, we're home.'

She seems bewildered as we escape to the shadowy corridors and I return her to her seat in reception.

'I bought a present for you in the city,' I say and dig into the bottom of my bag for the small, square box wrapped in Christmas paper that was intended for a friend: a ceramic container filled with potpourri.

She chuckles quietly and presses it to her chest.

'I have to go now,' I say and take a step backwards. She doesn't register my departure, simply sits in her chair in reception holding her gift.

36

A Club on the Water and a Dream of a Car Accident

Due to work pressure, it's two weeks since I've seen him. Needless to say, I'm feeling guilty. But perhaps he hasn't even noticed my absence. Or perhaps, if he has, he doesn't care. Either way, I feel the need to do something with him that he might enjoy. Maybe take him somewhere near the water again – a place that was once important to him, like the St George Motor Boat Club on Kogarah Bay, although it's further than we've ever been before.

The only problem is the possibility of having to take him to the men's toilet. And what if his bag needs emptying? Fiddling with his catheter is not something I would feel at all comfortable doing. Wouldn't it just be easier to sit quietly in the home's dining room or out in the courtyard, leaving the job of attending to leaks and full bags to the experts? But then he wouldn't get to enjoy the magnificent view over the bay where he spent much of his life.

I take the chance.

*

The Club was like a second home to my parents. They often went there on Fridays to have lunch together at their special table by the window in the St Kilda Room. It was also where Dad often moored his boat and spent the night, and from where he and his boating fraternity raced in time trials north to Port Stevens or south to Port Hacking.

I was with him once on his return from one of those races.

It was a miserably hot day as we left the Royal Motor Yacht Club and made our way slowly towards the Port Hacking estuary. As Dad steered north for Cape Solander and the entrance to Botany Bay, the weather broke. Bruised clouds were massing far to the south, slouching low over the horizon, and the sea had turned granite grey. He said not to worry, that we would easily outrun it and be safely at our moorings when it hit. But the day disintegrated as the front raced towards us. He was wrong for once, and I was no longer confident in his ability to handle the growing swell. The ocean heaved and skeins of rain hid the sandstone cliffs along the coastline. He laughed almost with contempt. I was not sure if it was at me cowering on the steps to the cabin or at what nature threw at him. He seemed to be enjoying his battle to control the boat every time it slumped into a deep trough with a heavy clunk and then teetered on the rim of the next swell before plummeting again. Eventually, the headlands of Botany Bay appeared out of the veil of rain, and he turned west, surfing the waves that ran through the entrance.

Despite all the years of my parents' fun-filled domestic and overseas travel and the plethora of luxury hotels, I would lay a bet on Dad's preference for taking his cruiser up the river or out into the bay, anchoring in some secluded cove with his girl, pouring a Scotch or two or three, and watching the sun go down, rocked to sleep by the sound of waves lapping against the hull.

Nothing would be more fun to Dad than a gathering of small and large cruisers, all anchored somewhere like Cattle Duffers Flat up the western end of the Georges River, out at Towra on the southern side of Botany Bay, or even at the Basin in Pittwater, and the camaraderie of sharing a meal, a drink, a game of cards, and a good laugh. I would bet that, rather than boarding a plane to some exotic location, he would have preferred to don his captain's cap and, with friends as crew, motor far beyond Cape Banks and Cape Solander for a day's deep-sea fishing.

*

He shuffles to the car, opens the passenger-side door, and stands aside to let me get in. 'No, Dad, it's okay. I'm driving today,' I say. 'Here, let me help *you*.' The seat belt seems slightly easier to get over his belly than the last time we went out.

From middle age, he'd developed a keg-like gut – 'relaxed muscle', he used to call it – which he invited his male grandchildren to punch as hard as they could. Like Harry Houdini, he believed in his own strength and ability to withstand pain, and when their clenched fists made no impression on the iron-like muscles, he'd laugh and say, 'You'll have to do a lot better than that.' They were determined to get the better of him one day, but I can't remember if or when they ever did.

This time, we cross the Georges River via the Taren Point Bridge and approach the club through the back streets of Sans Souci. I glance at him. He's running his tongue over his lips; they look dry and cracked, and I wonder if he's dehydrated. I won't offer him wine this time, but I must get him to drink water or some juice with his lunch, even if it means putting some strain on his bladder and possibly having to empty his bag.

We find a spot in the shade on the open terrace looking out at the state-of-the-art marina. Unlike the last few cruelly overheated days, today is milder; the water is glassy and the sky is translucent, with just a few high streaky clouds.

I go to the bar, get myself a wine and Dad a freshly squeezed orange juice and water, and then order Kilpatrick oysters for him. 'Okay?' I ask. He shrugs.

'Dad, I think you need to have some fluid,' I say and push the glass of juice closer to his hand resting on the table – a hand very similar to mine, with similar stocky fingers.

'That one's got two donks,' he says, pointing to the huge luxury cruiser berthed immediately in front of us. It seems that sometimes an image briefly catches his attention, as if hooked on a snag in a river, only then to be released to float away downstream.

He struggles with the oysters and drinks only half his juice. I wonder if I should relent and get him a wine. 'Want anything from the bar?' I ask.

'No love,' he says, and I leave him sitting staring out at the water, or at the cruiser with the two donks, or somewhere further away. I wish I knew where he went.

While I wait for my drink, having decided I can manage two and still drive safely, I allow my mind to wind back once again to the days when Dad would turn up at the club after Mum's View Club meetings. I often wondered if she liked him doing that. But perhaps she thought how lucky she was – as her friends often told her – to have such a caring husband. Although their relationship was the envy of others, I always thought it lacked space and freedom to allow them to develop other sides to their personalities.

I return to Dad, and we sit quietly. There's an explosive burst of success from the gaming room, and other sounds swell to fill the space between us: the murmur of a boat engine, the low growl of traffic somewhere in the distance, the screech of a fearless gull, a fly buzzing around Dad's head, and his own heavy breathing.

He continues to stare out at the water, the cruiser with the two donks reflected in his glasses. I am trapped in a grey sadness as I watch the man beside me wasting away – the man I admired so much, but also, over the years, felt such anger and resentment towards. There's a lump of guilt at many of my past feelings about him – but as he always said, guilt is a bloody, pointless emotion.

His thin voice breaks into my thoughts. 'That one's got two donks,' he reminds me.

'Yes, it's a fine cruiser, Dad.'

He smiles. Perhaps he thinks it belongs to him.

'I brought my girl here,' he adds, five words that pierce my heart.

'I know, Dad, many times.'

*

233

As my father slowly fades away, I am finding it hard to sleep and focus on the minutiae of my day-to-day life.

To revitalise myself, I walk most mornings through the Domain into the botanical gardens and along the harbour foreshore. I join a gym in the Grace Hotel, hoping by doing some resistance training to avoid the osteoporosis that plagued Mum. She didn't do much exercise in the second half of her life except the lifting of a glass of Scotch on the rocks and an occasional breaststroke lap of the pool, making sure she didn't get her hair wet. Over the weeks, pounding the paths down past the duck pond in the gardens, around to the opera house, Circular Quay, the Rocks, and back up Kent Street to my unit, I try being in the present instead of sliding back through the decades.

*

A dream has awakened me, a dream of an accident: a shattered vehicle, splattered blood, a lolling head. But I can't see the face. Oh my God! The boys! My heart drills against my ribs and my gut twists and knots just as it did all those years ago when they were teenagers, out late, out drinking and driving or being driven home. While the warm morning sun struggles to spike through the blinds, there's a cold terror inside every cell of my body. I will remain paralyzed, unable to function properly, until I check that all three sons are safe.

Adam answers. There's a lot of background noise; he's probably out with friends somewhere in Los Angeles. Josh is fine, already at work at Manly, lording it over the kitchen staff. Ben's the worry, though. I leave a text hoping he'll answer as soon as he wakes. He's probably in a loud snoring stupor after a night at the local sports bar in Manila's Makati. But on my way to the gym, he texts that everything is okay.

'You look a bit frazzled,' says Mike, the trainer on duty. He's adjusting the first apparatus. I'm the only one in the gym.

'Had a nasty dream about a car accident early this morning. Thought it might have been about one of my sons,' I explain as I start my stretches: standing on one leg and bending the other up behind me, pulling it back to touch my butt. 'But then, maybe it's about me? Aren't people in dreams often aspects of ourselves?' I ask. I roll my right arm over my shoulder and clasp my left hand behind my back, then reverse the action.

'I'm not *au fait* with dreams,' he says.

I lean forward with both arms outstretched to touch the wall and wonder if it's a premonition. I stand, bend over at the waist, and place the palms of my hands flat on the floor, remaining there for a few seconds before slowly unfurling. 'I seem to be obsessed lately with death: my father's, mine, and everyone else I care for,' I tell Mike.

'What if we give the apparatus and treadmill a miss today? Go outside. Do some vigorous walking for an hour. A walking meditation.'

As soon as I agree, he's off, legs pumping, pacing it out. I struggle to keep up. He disappears among the shoppers and office workers, reappears, jogs on the spot at the red light at George Street, then heads up King. Anything negative mulling around in my mind has no time to register as I weave in and out of the crowds. I feel ridiculous in my gym gear among the young corporate women in tight short skirts and jackets, flesh-coloured stockings, and black pumps – a look I have always hated, a uniform that speaks to me of ruthless, or futile, ambition.

At Queens Square, barristers in their wigs and flowing black gowns forge ahead of young solicitors heaving folders of court papers, some hauling their valuable documents in small airline trolley cases. I begin to breathe more easily as we enter Hyde Park, one of many green refuges in the heart of Sydney, but my heart clutches as we stride past homeless old men – and some not so old – huddled on benches and in little bushy dugouts surrounded by black plastic garbage bags containing their worldly possessions. I'd like to give them a few dollars but I hurry on: a kind of walk/run to catch up to Mike way ahead. He's stopped halfway down the cathedral-like aisle of trees, exercising on one of the seats scattered along its length. There's the sound of a siren nearby. I flinch and am back with the dream.

Near the crossing in Park Street, there's been an accident: two crumpled cars, police, and an ambulance.

'Come on,' Mike suggests, 'we'll go this way.'

'No, I've had enough, Mike. You go. I'm staying.'

I'm not usually an accident voyeur – I like to get away from such scenes – but I need to see if there's a lolling head and blood. Childish, I know.

'There's no point,' Mike insists. 'Come, I'll buy you a juice.'

'No, I'm staying.'

He throws me the kind of look that parents give recalcitrant children, and then he's off. 'Okay, see you next week.'

I stand back against the bushes of the park while ambulance officers try to extricate one of the drivers and a policeman with a notepad questions the other. The driver of the first car, hit from behind, is slowly helped to the back of the ambulance. The second driver is given a breath test.

As I leave the scene and wander across the diagonal path leading back to Elizabeth and Market Streets, a door to the past opens, and I hear the thrump of metal on brick.

Dad had come plummeting down the steep cement drive of Stuart Street out of control on the ride-on mower – a surprising brake failure – and hurtled into the rendered brick wall near the garage. He was dazed, his head fallen to one side, his leg slashed from knee to ankle, blood oozing around the pedals. He uttered no sound while he waited stoically for an ambulance to arrive.

I make my way back to the flat through the city crowd, focussing on the elements of the dream, trying to intuit its meaning. But it's not until I dig out a dream book hidden away on my bookshelves that I gain some real insight into it.

Accidents: 'Any dream of an accident indicates pent-up guilt for which you are subconsciously punishing yourself.'

Car accidents: 'To dream of a car accident symbolizes your emotional state, an emotional loss of control. You may be harboring deep anxieties and fears.'

Blood: 'Blood reflects emotional pain in waking life, a painful situation that is sapping your strength.'

*

The following day, I continue to lie in bed after my husband leaves for work. I'm lethargic, despite my recent exercise regime, and emotionally fragile, close to tears. I curl up into a question mark and try going back to sleep, but as usual my mind, when stuck on something, will not release me.

Around ten o'clock, I drag myself out of bed, leaving it unmade, and ring my friend Helen for a bit of emotional support.

'Don't forget to nurture yourself,' she says.

'But it's not as if I'm Dad's carer,' I tell her. 'I do very little for him. It's my sister-in-law who thinks more like a carer, and it's the staff who look after him.'

'But it's *your* emotional attachment to him that's exhausting you. Take some time off from all the analysing, Pam.'

Is it possible to wear oneself out from thinking too much?

For that is what I have been doing since we brought Dad Down South. Trying to hold onto him, to remember how he once was, to understand my feelings about him over the years – to discover something that I was too blind, distracted, or just plain uncaring to see before.

Part 3

Towards the West

37

Departures and Letting Go

No one yet fills the space previously occupied by Mary and John Gardner in the lunchroom. Their absence is not mentioned, but Mary's death has upset me more than I would have imagined, considering I never knew her as she once was and I only spoke to John occasionally. I wonder how long before Dad's spot will be vacant and what the pain will be like for me when his time comes.

I'm concerned that I've brought nothing with me to stimulate him and haven't planned any outing because I have to leave earlier than usual for a meeting. After lunch, we take a gentle walk. I make only the occasional comment and refrain from filling in the long periods of silence between us with questions, encouraging him to remember.

Maybe – just maybe – I've become a little more comfortable with the silences since the day with Harriet. But I don't think Dad and I are quite ready for the bus stop yet.

*

One week later.

Up ahead, a siren wails and a light flashes red. An ambulance negotiates the roundabout just before the entrance to the nursing home. I pray it drives on, but it turns left into the home's driveway and pulls up outside the main entrance. I screech to a stop in the underground car park and stumble up the stairs. A knife is jabbed into my gut.

Craig is rushing through reception. I grab his arm. 'Is it Dad, Craig?' I ask.

'No, Pam, it's not Greg. Must go.'

I flop into Harriet's chair outside the admin office to let the racing of my heart slow down. Could it be another one of the residents who spend their lunchtimes with Dad?

But of course. Harriet! I'm sitting in the chair she always occupies at this time of day. Why isn't she here? Is it her, that little fragile bird? My throat swells.

There are sounds of activity up the corridor: the rattle of the wheeled stretcher trolley, voices turned down low. The paramedics appear, calmly professional, one hurrying ahead to open the back door of the ambulance, the other negotiating the corridor corner. Craig is helping with the portable oxygen supply unit and a nurse is softly reassuring the patient, her face – for she is a female – hidden under an oxygen mask.

But the figure on the stretcher is not Harriet; it's a bigger woman with ash-brown hair.

Dad smiles wanly as I greet him in the rec room. Thank God there are no more absentees, only the empty space once filled by Mary in her wheelchair and her doting husband, John.

After lunch, Dad and I retire to the courtyard, but we don't speak. I don't want to; there's too much going on in my mind. How can the nurses and aides work in a place like this with its constant emergencies and inevitable departures? How do they steel themselves against such never-ending reminders of their own mortality?

Craig has come looking for me. 'Pam, can you leave Greg for just a moment?' I pat Dad on the knee, excuse myself, and follow him inside. 'I wasn't sure if you knew about Harriet,' he said. 'You seemed to have taken an interest in her, so I thought you'd like to know that she died peacefully in her sleep last Saturday.'

'Oh Craig,' I say, my voice already filled with tears. 'The poor, lonely little thing. I think I knew something was wrong when she wasn't in her usual seat.'

'A good way to go, though,' he answers.

'But she had no one. Who was there to organise or go to her funeral?'

'We tried contacting the only number we had, but it's disconnected; she's been in here so long. Her records showed that there was a plot in the Woronora cemetery paid for over twenty years ago. So we got in touch with a funeral place we sometimes use, and a few of the staff saw her off.'

I'm weeping openly by now. Weeping for little Harriet and for all those who just disappear each day.

'Why don't you go to the rec room and make yourself a cuppa. I'll check on Greg,' he says.

Alone with my tea, I let the tears and mascara flow down my cheeks. And I remember an orange and black butterfly – the one associated with the freedom of the soul upon death – hovering around Harriet's halo of hair during my last bus trip with her on that stinking hot Christmas day.

*

On my way home, I make a detour and once more turn into the entrance of the Woronora cemetery and crematorium where Dad brought his girl that April Tuesday in 1996.

This time I *will* find Mum's plaque.

I wind my way to the administration building to get whoever is on duty to check their records, having already prepared a lie to account for not knowing my mother's location. But I needn't have worried. They aren't interested in anything personal – simply click on the computer, check the register list, and print it off:

> Name: Carlson Hazel Annie
> Type: Ashes
> Location: Palm Court – Rose garden 24 – 0054
> Date: 17/04/1996

As it turns out, I had been nowhere near it on my last search. It's just a tiny little plaque – all we amount to in the end – still shiny and easy to read: 'Hazel Annie Carlson, Dearest wife and mother, At Rest 17/4/96. Aged 74 years. Loved and Remembered.'

But there's a mistake. Someone's made a mistake. She was not seventy-four. She was seventy-five, just eighteen days short of her seventy-sixth birthday. I guess it really doesn't matter in the end, though.

The sun is on my back as I squat in front of her plaque breathing in the delicious perfume of roses and gardenias, and trying to experience something. I think of all the things she was in her life and everything she did for me, but no emotion surfaces. She's not there. Am I a hard-hearted bitch?

But when I see the small space reserved beside her, I am distraught. My throat struggles to hold back the sobs as I run my hands through the bare soil that will soon cover all that is left of my father, and all the things we didn't say and share.

Then unexpectedly, as I turn to leave, the grief I didn't express for Mum on that day seven years ago finally surges up from some deep inner place, pressing against my chest cavity, threatening to crack it open. 'Oh Mum, I'm so sorry.' I lean my head against the trunk of a tree and sob helplessly, mourning the mother I resented so often over the years for being Dad's perfect princess.

*

Dad's decline has been the state in which I've been living for the past six months, and I need a break, a distraction, a forced separation.

'Letting go for a while doesn't mean you stop caring,' Helen said when I rang to ask her advice about the prospective three-week writing workshop on the Italian Amalfi Coast.

'But what if he dies while I'm away?'

'People are not always around when a loved one dies.'

'I know that, Helen. I was overseas when Mum passed away. And it's taken me until a few weeks ago to come to terms with the grief I didn't really express for her at the time.'

'Look, your dad could linger on for years,' Helen points out. 'Why don't you discuss the trip with the staff and talk to his doctor, just to make sure he's okay before you leave.'

I know what the doctor will say about the aneurism – that it could rupture at any time – but they have been saying that for about five or six years now. Maybe it *will* be okay. It's only for three weeks.

But how will I feel if he does die while I'm in Italy? How big the guilt and the grief?

A grey sludge-like misery washes over me at the thought of having to tell him. Two days before my departure, I visit him, wondering if in the years to come I'll say, 'The last time I saw my father was on a day in early April, just before I selfishly took off overseas.'

After lunch, I take him for a walk around the perimeter of the property, wondering if he's left any instructions about his wishes when he dies. I didn't find anything of the sort when I cleaned out his filing cabinets in Murwillumbah, but maybe my brother would know.

I hold him by the wrist, feeling the pulse of his flickering life. I notice the fine grey whiskers on his cheeks that, out in the strange afternoon light, give him a deathlike pallor. Is it possible he's just biding his time patiently until he can join Mum? But I'm not sure if he has any spiritual centre, or a belief in an afterlife. I've never heard him question why we are here or require answers to the great philosophical questions. Does he fear his own extinction?

'Dad,' I say, 'I won't be able to see you for a few weeks. I'm going to be out of the country for about twenty-one days. Italy.'

'Good, love,' he replies. I experience a profound sadness.

'So I won't be visiting for a few weeks,' I repeat. The silence elongates, and I don't know where to go from here.

'Are you waiting for me to give you permission?' he asks, his voice weak. Even at this stage, he continues to surprise me.

'Yes,' I say, like a child.

'Then go.' Of course, he would never say, 'I might not be here when you come back' – would never play that manipulative game.

'Dad, I love you,' I say as I guide him back to the warmth of the rec room.

'You think I don't know that.'

38

Contemplation at 9,000 Metres

I board the Singapore Airline flight with trepidation – fearful not only of the possibility of Dad's death while I'm away but also of my own mortality.

Before settling down in seat 34A, I check out the nearest emergency exit. When the engines roar, readying for take off, I ask 'it' – who or whatever 'it' is, God, universal energy, the source – to protect my father and myself for the next three weeks. Then I close my eyes and mentally 'help' the pilot lift the great bird off the ground. Not until I hear the clunk of the wheels returning to their housing do I open my eyes. Below me is the grey-blue expanse of Botany Bay, once Dad's boating playground.

We hit our first patch of turbulence about two hours out of Sydney. The seat belt signs light up, my gut seizes up, and my arms strangle the pillow I always keep on my lap as the plane bumps and shakes and the overhead lockers rattle. Unlike most on board, I'm unable to become absorbed in a movie or music. I'm afraid if I use the headphones I might miss out on an important message from the cockpit or stewards' intercom.

Somewhere over the red ochre heart of Australia, with its network of dried up watercourses and sparse vegetation, I wonder why I've avoided talking to Dad about dying or death – the big D, that great obscenity of Western society, a word most of us find difficult to say and for which we've found numerous euphemisms or slang substitutes to minimise its unpleasantness.

After our meal trays have been removed, I test myself to see how many alternatives to the word *dying* I can think of: passed (and passed over, passed on, passed away), gone to a better place, gone to one's reward, gone to meet one's maker, taken the last bow, cashed in one's chips, croaked, kicked the bucket, bitten the dust, fallen off the perch, and snuffed it. On a separate page, I try remembering literary references like 'shuffled off this mortal coil' and 'crossed the river Styx'.

Pointless, maybe, but it fills in the time. I order a gin and tonic, put aside my notebook, and try to get my thoughts off death by reading. But the only thing to read, apart from the *Guardian* newspaper – with its chilling reports of violence in Iraq – is the inflight magazine, *SilverKris*. I dig out *Foucault's Pendulum* by Umberto Ecco, a massive tome I started weeks before. It's hard going, like wading through mud in heavy boots, filled as it is with historical references, allusions, endless dialogue, and background material. Hardly a good choice for a flight. Instead, I browse through the glossy magazine with its adverts of beautiful people in exquisite pieces of jewellery and more beautiful people urging the purchase of exorbitantly priced perfumes. I turn to an article on the world's most exclusive spa resorts and read a few paragraphs, and then I return the magazine to the front pocket along with the menus, unused headphones, sick bag, newspaper, and novel.

The pilot announces that there is an area of intense turbulence somewhere ahead over the Banda Sea, and I am thrown back to thoughts of death. What would it be like to hurtle to one's death from 9,000 metres? Would one be unconscious or aware until the plane slammed into the sea or a mountainside? How do people face their own impending deaths?

And is there such a thing as a good death?

Some people might say a good death is to just fall asleep and never wake up. If that's the case, then Mum had a good death. But is that the best thing for those left behind, unable to say goodbye? Others might think it would be better to have some warning so that they can prepare, become intimate with their fears, model a peaceful acceptance, and take the dying process as a blessing. There's no doubt such preparation and acceptance would certainly be a gift to those left behind. Still others might think it preferable to be unaware of their impending demise, like Harriet. Of course, I don't really know if she had a sense of death approaching.

And what is Dad thinking? Or is he not thinking much at all?

If I still had my mind and knew I had limited time, I'd like to give death my absolute attention and plan a rite of passage for myself that hopefully provides a transformative journey for those who care about me. But who knows; I might just slide into a fighting or frightened decline, or an 'it's so unfair' ranting.

By the time we approach Singapore's Changi Airport, I have unwisely consumed several gin and tonics and a red wine. Despite my relief when we touch down, I have five hours to fill before the next leg to Rome. To get my circulation going, I wander aimlessly along the endless arteries leading from the terminal hubs and have a foot massage. I need to get inebriated enough to relax but not so drunk that I'll miss my flight. I find a corner in Harry's Bar, order something called a Sparkling Sziget at $15 Singaporean per glass, and listen appreciatively to a Singaporean vocalist singing the hits of my favourite early 1970s soft-rock group Bread. Finally, I hop the series of travelators to Gate Whatever with still an hour before boarding and grab a quick relax in a vibrating chair opposite the boarding gate.

Despite having consumed three of Harry's Sparkling Szigets, I don't sleep once on board as we head west following the setting sun. The second leg is just as rough as the first, and we are required to be strapped in for long stretches.

So for hours, sitting cramped up in economy, I allow my mind to spool backwards, triggered by a statement made by Belbo, one of the characters in *Foucault's Pendulum,* about his childhood: 'What we become depends on what our fathers teach us at odd moments, when they aren't trying to teach us. We are formed by little scraps of wisdom.'

I search my memories for anything Dad said or did that might have had an influence on me when he wasn't actually teaching me. Most of his 'scraps of wisdom' were expressions, like, 'Work it out for yourself', 'Don't sell yourself short or settle for less', 'Don't rely on others', 'Deal with it, try it again, give it a go', 'Don't expect handouts',

'Stop whingeing', 'Don't take any crap', and 'Use your bloody common sense'.

But it was more than what he said; it was the way he behaved: the 'show don't tell' of life: how he handled himself under stress and approached all kinds of challenges and setbacks; his willingness to take risks, never giving up until he had reached his goal; how he took responsibility for all his choices whether they turned out to be good or bad, never blaming others for what happened; his aversion to snobbery; and his continuing generosity to friends and strangers alike. And then there was the way he behaved with his kids. He didn't see the necessity of being friends with us. His role, as he saw it, was to protect us, teach us everything he knew, discipline us, and help us have a better life than he had. What could be better for a child than that?

By the time we make our approach to Rome's Fiumicino–Leonardo da Vinci International Airport, I know without a doubt that Dad always wanted the best for me even as an adult, despite his sometimes strange ways of showing it.

39

Still With Me

During my long wait for the rest of the writing group at the Rome airport, I buy and skim a copy of Shirley Hazzard's short book *Greene on Capri,* about her friendship with the English novelist Graham Greene. But damn it! I can't get away from Dad. I see him in Hazzard's description of her friend's 'unappeasable spirit'; his prickly, volatile, and cantankerous personality; and his generous and complex character.

*

The domestic flight to Naples is nightmarish as we toss around in mountainous banks of roiling clouds with no sight of land until we break through into the Neapolitan pollution. And I know there's one more challenge before we reach our destination, because I've faced it several times before – when I was much younger and without fear. It is the narrow, precipitous road from Sorrento along the coast, winding between mountain slopes on one side and a sheer drop into the abyss of the Tyrrhenian Sea on the other. It is spectacularly beautiful and breathtaking, but not for the faint-hearted if the traffic is heavy.

In 1953, the writer John Steinbeck experienced this drive and wrote in an essay that the high narrow road 'hooked and corkscrewed on the edge of nothing', and that he and his wife in the back seat of a car 'lay clutched in each other's arms weeping hysterically'.

'What a wuss,' Dad would have said of Steinbeck, and in my imagination I can see him relishing the challenge of constantly backing up to avoid the buses going in each direction, pulling to the side of the road mere centimetres from a sheer drop, and dealing with the maniacal Vespa riders with a death wish.

I'm at a window seat as our bus teeters on the edge of the vertical limestone sea cliffs and – as in the plane during turbulence – my breathing is shallow, pincers squeezing my gut. I avoid looking out over the vertigo-inducing vista of azure sea, focussing ahead on the jumble of pastel-coloured houses, churches, and terraced gardens tumbling down the mountain flanks.

Eventually, the bus grinds to a halt in the little village of Praiano close to the sixteenth-century church of San Genarro with its shining dome and cupola of cobalt blue, white, and yellow glazed earthenware tiles. Once out of the bus, I am hit with the blaze of bougainvillea in neon pinks and reds, the heady fragrance of lemon, and the aromatic perfume of myrtle. At last … maybe I can relax.

Waiting for our arrival is Rafaello, the elder son of the hotel owner. We find him leaning against a stone balustrade, waiting to help with our luggage. 'Look at me!' his stance demands: well-developed torso, one leg slightly bent, a hand on his hip, and a small section of his T-shirt tucked into his jeans. He hoists the first pieces of our luggage onto his shoulders and carries them down the approximately ninety steps to the hotel – for Praiano, like all villages and towns along the coast, consists of winding alleyways and endless steps.

Mario, Rafaello's dark curly-haired father, greets us with welcoming drinks in what I come to call the green room, and I recognize something of a younger Dad in the hospitable Italian. The room's olive, avocado, and leafy greens are offset at one end by a bird in a yellow cage and terracotta urns containing cheery yellow and cerise blooms. At the other end are a stuffed tiger; two stone lions; paintings of the family dog and Catholic saints; and a poorly executed replica of the Venus de Milo. Green half-shells camouflage the wall lights, and numerous ceramic lamps create a more subdued effect. It is Mario's Italian version of the Stuart Street rumpus room where he is the king of his castle.

There is no mistaking the family's connection to the sea. Prominently featured on one side of the room are two glass cases containing replicas of ships, a picture frame displaying nautical knots, and a miniature life buoy with a chronometer at its centre and 'Welcome Aboard' printed on its rim. When Mario leads us out to the extensive tiled and plant-filled terrace, pointing with pride to his small cruiser moored in the cove below, I know he has Dad's love for boating.

Once settled into my room in the Villa Bellavista, with its wide patios and views over the Sorrentine peninsula and across to Capri, I phone the family with my new contact number. Dad is okay, apparently, and I'm hoping I can wind down over the following weeks as we walk in the footsteps of some of the literary greats who came to reside – some temporarily, some permanently – in this beautiful part of Italy.

*

There is a steady drumming above my bed. It's around six in the morning, and the light is still dim. Outside, water gushes from the main road down the side stairs and through the terraced gardens to the small beach way below. Everything beyond 100 metres or so is drained of colour – just tones of grey, not the early morning palette of postcard blues, whites, and pastels I'd expected. Charcoal cliffs loom out of murky mica waves, the sky hangs heavily, and squalls obscure the Sorrentine peninsula and the three thrusting islands of Li Galli. Hopefully this is just an isolated spring shower.

Mario repeatedly apologises as if he is somehow responsible, and we are unable to hold our workshop on the spacious terrace as planned. Instead we are forced to wait for the breakfast tables to be cleared so that we can use the dining room.

About eleven o'clock, there's a pause in the rain. The wind and swell ease, and the clouds shred like a worn sheet, allowing shafts of light to penetrate and adding a silver sheen to sea and cliffs – a sign of hope. But not just yet! Further squalls veil the cliffs and islands, and a lone fishing boat flounders in the maelstrom of breakers just off the stone watchtower, one in a series built along the coast to repel Turkish and Saracen marauders in the thirteenth century.

For one of our first writing exercises, we are each handed a black and white photo to describe. But it's just what I don't need: an image of four old men sitting together on a bench in the sun outside a café. It reminds me of Keats's words from *Ode to a Nightingale* – 'Here where men sit and hear each other groan; Where palsy shakes a few, sad, last grey hairs' – and of the old men sitting with Dad in the nursing home rec room in North Wing.

But the old men in my photo appear to have some life left in them still. Two of them stare straight ahead, another scratches his head, and the remaining one has his face screwed up to focus on someone or something just out of the shot. The two in the centre of the picture have their legs crossed, and cigarettes dangle from their fingers; the other two wear the flat cloth caps popular with old men in southern Italy or working class English towns. All four are dressed in lace-up shoes, long pants, jumpers, and zippered cardigans. There are no walking frames or hovering nurse's aides.

For my creative exercise, I try imagining a life for 'my men' among caring extended families and a community of friends, so different from my father, who sat alone for seven years in the sun Up North without his shirt and – by choice – without the support of family and close companions.

40

The Changing Moods of Praiano

In the afternoon, there's a brief break in the weather, and I tackle the ninety steps to the Piazza San Gennaro with its ochre-coloured parish church dedicated to the martyred third-century Neapolitan bishop Januarius. I'm forced to stop frequently to regain my breath, but an old couple, sharing an umbrella, pass me with a '*buon giorno*'. They climb the stairs with the agility of mountain goats and soon disappear from sight.

The piazza is a communal gathering place, Mario told us, used for community festivals, predominantly religious, as well as by Praiano boys for soccer. But today, the square is empty except for Saint Gennaro with his back to the sea and Jesus and Mary with their backs to the mountains. The rain starts again; I seek shelter in a doorway near the bell tower, but it offers little protection. The downpour whips up into my face. I try the church's heavy bronze door, and it opens easily. Barely discernible in the muted light, a lone figure kneels in the front pew, head bowed.

On the best of days I'm not one for churches and their religious icons – their suffering Christs, relics, ornate altars, candelabra, and votive offerings. But on this wet, blustery afternoon, I ease into a pew close to the door and, for a brief moment, consider saying a prayer for my father to still be there when I return.

Instead, my mind turns to my grandfather Bertrand. Strange, you might think, since he's been dead for thirty-six years. Dad's father had a stroke just before I left for England in 1965, and I believed I'd never see him again. But he managed to survive until I returned, and he was able to see his great-grandson a week before he died. Can people really do that if their desire is strong enough?

The lone figure at the front of the church rises, moves out into the aisle, makes obeisance before the altar, and turns. It is the woman who passed me on the stairs earlier with her husband. Has she been praying for a sick or absent loved one, seeking solace for some grief she has experienced, or just giving thanks for the blessings in her life? As she passes, she smiles, creating deep furrows in her old cheeks and highlighting the sun-wrinkled skin around her eyes. She probably thinks I'm here to worship, but the empty church feels cold and oppressive, and I leave.

It's still raining heavily as I sprint across the square to the main road and enter the Bar del Sol – how ironic, I think.

It is filled with old men, cigarette haze, and two well-fed white cats. Worn pouches of tobacco lie discarded on tables, and thin roll-your-own cigarettes dangle from mouths and stained fingers. Some of the men huddle in groups over chess or chequer boards or cards, occasionally breaking their intense concentration with loud outbursts. I'm not sure if they are arguing or if they're deaf. Perhaps it's just the normal volume of Italian conversations, or maybe they've raised their voices to compete with the pelting rain outside. I order a carafe of the local red wine and settle in to wait.

Suddenly, the bell in the church tower across the road clangs into life. Its toll is grim and foreboding, reminding me of 'for whom this bell tolls' from *Devotions Upon Emergent Occasions* by John Donne, the sixteenth century English poet: 'Perchance he for whom this bell tolls may be so ill, as that he knows not it tolls for him.'

The old blokes in the cafe push back their chairs and, braving the rain, shuffle down the front steps and across the road in a parade of black umbrellas to what I assume is an afternoon Mass; men of a simple but firm devotion. I wonder if their daily lives are profoundly comforted by their religion. Does their fervent faith help them cope with thoughts of death, or will they, when their time arrives, be afraid?

Would I be less depressed if I knew Dad had a strong spiritual faith?

The rain eases, but I remain where I am, finishing off my carafe. When it finally stops, I go for a walk up past the grocery store to a little square with only one small bench and a cement railing where a few old ladies have gathered. I pass a house with what appears to be a death notice attached to the front door, judging by the only words I can identify – *decesso* and *funerale* – and then wind my way to Praiano's austere main church dedicated to St Luke the Evangelist. A funeral crowd is gathered outside, and the first of the pallbearers – the man who passed me on the stairs – appears in the church doorway.

I don't hang around; the rain still threatens, and I am too caught up in my own cheerless thoughts.

Back in my room, I have to steel myself against ringing home and checking on Dad.

*

Finally the sun returns to Praiano, and the gloomy mood that enveloped me lifts. In fact, everyone has lightened up as we gather on the sunny terrace to begin another day of writing. Along the coast, Positano glistens like a waterfall, and in the distance, jewel-like Capri and the three islands – legendary home of the Sirens who lured sailors to their deaths – shine in a sea streaked with turquoise and lapis. Below us, lacy patterns of foam have formed close to shore, and cypresses stand like sentinels against a ceramic sky. Silvery olives, their gnarled trunks like the old Praiano men, bend to the soil. And then there are the fruit trees with their abundant, full-bodied blood oranges and lemons glowing in the April sun wherever a small amount of land and soil allows.

With the sun come the sounds: the chirrups of birds, the buzz of bees, and the purring of the fat communal cats lazing on sun-warmed terracotta tiles; the laughter of children echoing down the stairways as they return to their games in the piazza or race home for lunch; and the calls of women gathered on landings between consecutive flights of stairs. Up in the main street, the shop proprietors shout greetings to passers-by and older adolescent boys return to their preening and perving position among the Vespas opposite the Bar del Sol, while the grizzled old men continue their discussions, games of cards, and chess on the bar's outdoor terrace, warming their old bones.

A community comes to life.

41

The Beginning of the End

Sydney experienced a relatively warm autumn while I was away, but just to make me feel really crap, on the day of my return to the nursing home, there is a shift in the quality of the air. Of course, autumn can be both cheerful and dismal. One moment, skies are crisp, clear, and blue, as gold, cinnamon, and russet leaves joyfully roll down the pavement or crunch underfoot like eggshells; the next, the weather turns melancholic, with grey skies occasionally perforated by ghosts of weak sunlight, chilly winds, thin drizzle, and slippery sodden leaves plastered to the pavement, a trap for the careless.

It is on the latter sort of day that I drive out to see my father after a break of over three weeks, a day when we will be forced inside. I pass Botany Bay, grey and choppy, its waves white-crested and menacing.

I put on some soothing music and turn my mind back to the days when the sun returned to Praiano – to the walks along ancient mountain paths between myrtle and broom; to the quiet meditations on Marcus Aurelius's spiritual reflections in a lemon grove, under a beech tree, or among wild irises growing beside an old cliff-side monastery; to the views from the heights of Ravello and Ana Capri; and even to getting a bit tipsy with new friends over a bottle of limoncello at the Bar del Sol.

But the closer I get to the nursing home, the more something sad and hopeless seems to linger in the air. It's reflected in the liquid ambers in the surrounding gardens and streets, almost bare of leaves, with just a few exhausted ones determinedly holding on.

*

I experience a charge of pain at how much he's aged in three weeks. His cheeks have fallen in, he has begun to slump within himself, and his eyes seem to have followed his mind to some faraway place. How fragile he's become. My heart clenches, and my throat burns. It is possibly the saddest day I can remember.

I take my seat next to him in the rec room and kiss him on his stubbled cheek. He nods to acknowledge my presence. Jack, the old bloke who sat opposite him at lunch, is not there, and there is someone else missing from the other end of the table. I am ashamed to say I don't remember who it is; all I know is that there are now two more empty places. And I don't like to ask about their absence.

The aides bring in the food, and I look at what is placed in front of Dad: raspberry jelly, small cubes of tinned fruit salad, and custard. No main course. I look to the aide for some explanation. 'That's all Greg seems to like now. He doesn't have much of an appetite these days.'

He picks up his spoon, his hand shaky, and makes an effort to lift the dessert to his mouth. Most of it falls off the spoon. After several attempts, I ask if he'd like me to feed him. He ignores my offer and perseveres.

When the lunch things are cleared away, we remain at the table. I place my hand over his, noting his papery skin, and tell him about my trip. I don't know if he remembers I went away, but it doesn't really matter. In a soft, slow voice I relate my story, making a big thing about Mario and his hospitality, his green room, his cruiser, and the boat trips to Capri and Amalfi, hoping for a flicker of interest when I mention the boat. But there's none.

I watch the quivering light play on the wall opposite, as I have often done before in moments of silence with him, and listen once again to the ticking of the clock. Then in a threadbare voice that lifts my heart, he says, 'Sounds good, darl.' He struggles to stand. 'Need to sleep now.'

I return him to the mausoleum-like South Wing and Room 22, where the other occupants appear to be asleep already, their raspy breathing punctuated by an intermittent pinging from somewhere outside. I settle Dad in his bed, kiss him lightly on the forehead, and tell him I love him. Within minutes, he has winged his way to another place, a more pleasant place than the one he has just left, I'm sure. I let a young aide know that he is in bed, but I really need to speak to someone in authority. Maybe I'll ring and make an appointment.

In reception, there is no one sitting in little Harriet's chair, and I'm pleased.

'Pam, you're back.' It's Craig's friendly voice.

'Yes, but I'm quite upset at Dad's deterioration.' I am immediately ashamed that my tone might be interpreted as accusatory.

He looks at his watch and asks, 'Have you got time for a quick chat?' His cheery voice has damped down somewhat.

'Sorry if I sounded a bit brusque.'

'Understandable.'

In the rec room, we sit on opposite sides of the table. 'Look, Craig, I'm really worried about Dad's sudden weight loss.'

'Not so sudden really, it's been happening gradually. I know you probably don't want to hear this, Pam, but I think your dad is preparing to go.'

I find it difficult to swallow and have to force myself to breathe. 'You mean he's getting close to death?'

'Well, I don't know just how *close* he is, but I think he's started his journey. Death is an active process among the elderly,' he says, his voice comforting, his face full of compassion. I've never heard people talk like this before. 'It's a very important time for old people,' he adds, 'but every path is different. Some take their time; others hurry it along. A bit like a baby's entry into the world.'

'So what do you think he might be going through right now?'

'Most people I've worked with in nursing homes and hospitals eventually come to a place where they finally accept that death will occur. That might be where he is now.'

'Has he ever said anything to you about dying?'

'Not exactly. I've never heard him say that he *wants* to die, but a few times he's said he'll be with his girl soon.' I rest my head in my hands, hoping to hell he will be. Craig doesn't push the conversation, just lets me take my time digesting what he's said.

'So you think he's started to leave?'

'Well, he's begun to exhibit some of the physical signs.' I wait for him to elaborate. 'He's more withdrawn than he was a few weeks ago. People approaching death generally withdraw more and more from their surroundings. They eat less and sleep more. I don't really know, but maybe it's their way of separating from this world in preparation for what comes next.'

'I had thought I might bring up the subject of dying with him, but I won't now of course. It's a relief really, as I don't think I'd be able to find the right words of comfort to deal with the terrible honesty of the subject.'

'It's hard for loved ones to know what to do for the best. Some think they are doing the right thing by trying to control the dying process.'

'How long does this go on for then?'

'As I've said, everyone's journey is different. It depends if they are just old or if there are other extenuating circumstances, but from my experience, a few weeks, a month, rarely as much as three.'

The tears start. 'I just want a bit more time with him.'

He comes around the table and places a gentle hand on my shoulder. 'Then take it. The last of the senses to go is hearing, so talk to him – even if he looks as if he's somewhere else.'

Craig leaves me there, and the floodgates open. By the time I drive away half an hour later, I am totally drained, my eyes red and swollen. The anticipatory grief that started when I first saw him living alone Up North all those years ago is coming to an end.

My trip away gave me the space I needed to look with new eyes at the mixed feelings I'd had for Dad over the years, and for my own peace of mind, I decide to share some of this with him. Whether he registers what I say or not, I know I must be truthful or else it will dishonour both of us. But it won't be easy; it will need a gentle honesty, and there must be no blame game, no wallowing in self-pity, no playing the victim, no expectations of something in return from him.

I begin visiting him more often and hope Craig was right, that even if he recedes more and more often into some place between worlds, my sentiments will reach him somehow.

As he becomes more emaciated, eats less, sleeps more, and moves in and out of lucidity, I sit with him, sometimes at the table in the rec room, sometimes beside his bed, stroking the wafer-thin skin on his hand and talking, allowing jumbled thoughts to fall from my lips like a stream of consciousness piece of writing.

During these after-lunch sessions – and they are like therapy sessions for me – I watch for signs that he hears what I am saying: a fleeting smile, a change in his eyes, the pressure of his hand. Although there are few verbal responses, I hope that some of what I say registers with him – but just in case, during each visit I tell him how much I admire and love him and how grateful I am to have had him as a father.

Sometimes I laugh and joke about many of his weird and quirky ways, sometimes I let the tears flow, and sometimes I develop an excruciating headache, like a skewer shoved in my forehead.

Somewhere among the tangled and disconnected babble are little anecdotes like the time he bought me a pair of running spikes when I was eight, even though there were none available that were small enough for my tiny feet, and how he stuffed the toes with newspaper so I could use them in the State Primary School Athletics Championships. And there are admissions after fifty years: my guilt in the Cadbury chocolate affair and how petrified I was when he threatened to call the police to identify the culprit by matching the tooth marks that he said were like fingerprints.

I elaborate on all the things I believe made him such a good father. Not the big things – like the weddings, parties, buying me a second-hand car when I was expecting my third child, or paying off what remained of our mortgage – but his continual attempts to give me new learning experiences. I talk about the great holidays, especially those where he encouraged us to get back to basics, and the challenges he set us to do the best we could, to be competitive and never give up trying.

I try explaining some of the things I didn't appreciate about him when I was young and how I have come to understand why he had done what he did. How I thought he'd been unduly harsh on me but maybe that was because I was the eldest and the most like him; how I'd developed a negative view of myself and blamed him for it, although I *was* probably a 'complete dill' in taking to heart many of the things he said; how he seemed to get pleasure from provoking me because I always overreacted; how it would have been nice occasionally to have received some compliments even though I knew he really was proud of me; how as an adult and mother, I understood his tough approach to discipline because children always need boundaries, and how I appreciated his insistence on manners and doing things properly.

I know I am taking a risk – evidenced by the throbbing in my forehead – as I admit how upset I felt when I thought he wanted me to be more like Mum as I got older, even though he must have known it was impossible since I had inherited many of his traits. His eyes, overlarge in his increasingly gaunt face, are watching me. Is it a warning to be careful, or is it simply my imagination? I can't prevent my voice from cracking when I finally admit that there were times when I resented her because she was something I could never be: someone's princess. Is there a hint of warmth in his eyes? I ask him what he would have said to me if I'd ever admitted that when I was younger. He shakes his head slowly, and I know exactly what he is thinking. I laugh and say, 'Yes, I know, Dad, a complete dill once again.' His mouth flickers into a half smile.

I take his hand and tell him she was a wonderful mother and how thankful I am that he loved her so much, because their love gave us a stable family.

I really hope he hears me.

*

Despite the sadness of his imminent death, a burden seems to have lifted, and I'm feeling more at peace than I have in a long time. Does it sound uncaring when I admit that I forked out for a bottle of Moët & Chandon, and that as I sat on my balcony in the city, watching the bubbles rise in the crystal flute and the setting sun turn the glass and steel buildings a molten gold, I raised the fizzing liquid to my lips and silently toasted both my father and myself?

42

A Winter Send-Off

The last time I ever see him is on a winter's day in early June 2004, the sky a faded blue, the pale and watery sun flickering through the naked branches in the grounds of Sutherland Hospital.

My brother had rung to say that Dad had been transferred from the nursing home suffering from a sudden fever and chills, nausea, vomiting, and severe abdominal pains due to an infection that his weak immune system was unable to cope with. It was septicaemia, apparently, a life-threatening infection that can get worse very quickly.

I loathe hospitals: their antiseptic smell, the glare of the nurse's stations, emergency gurneys echoing along corridors, and whispers from behind curtained beds. I can't really remember much about what I was thinking on that day when I found Dad's dimmed room with its one pale needle of light piercing the blinds. Maybe I was hoping that it would soon be all over for him, and for us of course, although we would yet have to face our own challenges.

His half-open but unseeing eyes, slack jaw, and the bluish tinge around his lips indicate he is slipping away fast, and I wonder just how much I will feel his absence in the coming weeks and years ahead. I suspect that most of all, I'll regret the fact that I never really got to know the heart of him – his innermost thoughts, hurts, and angers.

'I'm here, Dad,' I say and lay my hand on his forehead. In the gloomy stillness, I listen to his slow and irregular breathing that barely causes a movement of the blanket covering his body. Soon enough will come the death rattle. In contrast, my own breathing is rapid, and my heart hammers within my chest. Surprisingly, my eyes are dry.

I sit unmoving but allow my mind to wander.

There'll be no large gathering of family and friends encircling his bed to say goodbye; he'd hate that. But it would be great if there was something meaningful when he leaves, so I could say in years to come, 'At the moment my father took his last breath, I heard his favourite song playing somewhere in the distance', or 'When my father died, the clock in the hospital room stopped'. Better still would be something symbolically dramatic like a lightning bolt striking a power pole outside the hospital window and a total blackout. But maybe he'll wait to go at the exact moment of the upcoming Transit of Venus, that rare astronomical event – not seen by any human alive today – due in two days' time, the eighth of June.

The hours pass, and, as the circle of his life slowly closes, I remember what he said when Mum died: 'We all have to go through it. No point fussing about it.'

At one point, his mouth widens momentarily as if to take in more air, and I think this might be it, but then he moves his right arm from beneath the white hospital blanket, the palm of his hand facing up. I take it, stroking the transparent skin, fascinated by the myriad blue threads on the underside of his wrist. I need to say something now. I know he'll hear me. I'm tempted to tell him to let go, but I won't because I know he'll bloody well decide when to do that himself, and I suspect it will be when no one is around. So I simply tell him once again how grateful I am that he was my father and how much I really loved him.

And then I feel it and know.

He squeezes my hand with as much strength as he can muster, and I gently squeeze his in return: a memorable signing off, a moment to relive in years to come.

*

He survives that night and into the next day. There is obviously something else he needs to do. Perhaps it is the time spent with my brother who sits with him. But in the early evening, when Peter quickly returns home to have a shower and change, Dad leaves with no one to see him off, just as I suspected he would. His choice, I believe, like everything else in his life.

I read somewhere that we can use grief as a positive catalyst to become a stronger person. I don't know if it works like that for everyone, but I'm sure that's how Dad reacted to Mum's death after fifty-five years of marriage. And it's how I intend to treat his death, despite the emotional pull he always had on my heart. He would have expected us to mourn privately and briefly, but of course there is no guidebook for the proper way or length of time to grieve.

*

On the eleventh of June, the same day Ronald Reagan was buried in Washington, DC, we gather outside the South Chapel where we had seen my mother off eight years before. The light is alternately soft and hard, a fading in and out of the sun as small clouds drift across the sky. Dad lies in his coffin in the back of the hearse as people sign the book and make their way inside.

Among those present, I am moved to see Craig and Kylie from the nursing home, come to pay their respects to the man who kept them amused with his wacky sense of humour. I believe they had a genuine affection for Dad. There are others: some come out of obligation to my brother, sister, myself, and our families; a few are survivors from his former factory staff: one is an elderly man who made the trip via two trains from western Sydney; and there are a number from his Lions Club days, although many of his former friends and colleagues have gone now or are too incapacitated to attend.

I know most of those present will have their own stories about him, diverse perspectives that reveal things about him that I never knew. And just as many of them will not recognize the man I'll acknowledge later in my personal eulogy.

As his coffin is carried in to Frank Sinatra's 'I Did it My Way', *naturally*, I hear him from years ago commenting on the pointless expense of choosing a fancy coffin, something that is going to be burnt to a cinder. 'Don't waste your money on all that crap,' he'd said, meaning I suppose the very best timber, the bronze handles, and the silk linings. We chose a moderately expensive one and had it completely covered in native flowers, a decision made because we thought they suited Dad's personality: tough and adaptable, a survivor.

Someone sitting behind me touches my shoulder and says, 'He had a good run, didn't he?' I nod, but I want to say that it doesn't lessen the pain. Then just before the proceedings start, another person whispers jokingly, 'Your turn to step up to the plate now.' I ignore the comment, but it lingers, and I'm unsettled by its implication as the celebrant takes his place and reads the well-known but anonymous poem, 'The Measure of a Man':

> Not 'how did he die?'
> But 'how did he live?'
> Not 'what did he gain?'
> But 'what did he give?'
> These are the units of a man as a man
> To measure the worth regardless of birth …

In most of the funerals I've attended, I get the impression that the celebrant really wants to be centre stage – unfair, maybe, but it's the way I see their long-winded histories of the deceased that lack any personal sentiment. The celebrant we've chosen for Dad's send-off is a nice-enough man and highly competent at his job, but that's all it is: a bloody job. He never knew Dad and simply goes on in his boring voice, listing the main features of my father's life that we provided for him.

How often do members of families say, 'Oh, I couldn't get up and say anything, I'd break down'? Yes, I know some people don't like speaking in public, and some cannot help weeping copiously, but I'd much rather listen to an emotional acknowledgement from someone close. It usually avoids the complete fiction that many funerals celebrate.

My mouth dries out and my heart pounds as I take the dais. I want to raise my left hand as if holding a glass and say, 'Let's give a virtual toast to the complete man, the man with all his great attributes and his flaws, the man for whom I think *nice* was too mild a descriptive word, the man who wasn't particularly concerned with what people thought of him. But instead, I take a deep breath and start with, 'You'll all have your own memories and ways of describing Greg – some positive, some negative, I guess – so let's honour him for whatever he was to you.'

And I continue. 'I really don't know if Dad had any particular religious beliefs – it was something he never discussed with me – but one thing I am sure about is that he hoped in some way to be reunited with Mum. I would like to believe that we all have a brief human experience, rather like an actor playing a role in a play. There comes a time when we leave the stage, take off our costumes, and go home to wait for another role. If that is the case, then the play in which Dad starred had a relatively long and successful run.

'But it's not my father's successes I want to talk about. I would rather tell a few personal anecdotes that provide an insight into the man *I* knew.'

So long as I keep my eyes off my sister, sister-in-law, and several nieces who are crying, my voice remains strong. I relate a number of humorous anecdotes – well, funny in hindsight – and some of Dad's quirky ways, but when I reach the end, my voice falters. 'I hope Mum was waiting for him in the wings with a Scotch and water,' I say through my tears. 'Goodbye, you old bugger, we really loved you.'

Next comes an email sent from my eldest son, Adam, in the USA and read out by my middle son, Josh. After the initial preamble, Adam expresses what I'm sure would be a common sentiment felt by all Dad's grandchildren:

> Greg Carlson, what a life! Certainly full and varied from start to finish. A life to be proud of, and one that all of us can use as inspiration. Some of my fondest memories are of the summers at Stuart Street, whether it was messing around in the pool, or out on the boat, under the house exploring and raiding the fridge full of Coke and Fanta or woofing down BBQ'd sausages – fantastic days always ending with drinks in the rumpus room. Thanks Pop, I will miss you. Travel safely and give Hazel a kiss for me when you see her again. Love Adam.

Despite having held it together while I was required to speak, I am completely undone by this simple message from my son.

An acknowledgement from one of Dad's Lions Club friends is next: 'Greg was one of an elite breed of men who always had fun doing good deeds which made a difference in the lives of the sick, the elderly, and the needy. A man who truly gave of the three Ts: his time, his talent, and his treasure. He used to say that you never get giddy doing good turns … Greg and his princess also invented the word *hospitality*. Have you ever known anyone just having a couple of drinks at 114 Stuart Street? … I was also fortunate to share another aspect of Greg's life: boating. He initiated me into the world of "blue water" boating from the moment I participated in a life-changing trip to Port Stephens as a member of his crew in his savage cruiser … Mine and other lives have been made much richer by knowing this generous, fun-loving, and warm person.'

After a few moments of silence, the celebrant takes centre stage once more with a few homilies – moving, no doubt, when one is in an emotional state but ones I'm sure he includes in all his services – and then leads us in the Lord's Prayer as the curtain finally closes on Dad. But the celebrant is not finished yet. There are other comforting words he feels he must say: 'Since you have left us, our lives are not the same, so walk with us throughout our lives until we meet again.'

To the background – once again – of 'I Did it My Way', the celebrant announces, 'Greg's family have asked me to invite you to join them at the Royal Motor Yacht Club, Woolooware, for refreshments, a farewell toast, and to further reminisce. As Greg often said, the sun is always over the yardarm somewhere.'

*

The scattered clouds dissipate as we wind our way towards Cronulla and the Royal Motor Yacht Club on Port Hacking. By the time the guests, with full glasses in their hands, gather on the terrace with its sweeping views across Gunnamatta Bay, the day has become a clear winter blue.

I would like to think that Dad has not yet gone, for it would be a perfect send-off.

Perhaps he's out there somewhere on one of the gleaming cruisers, wearing his white shirt with the commodore-like epaulettes, his captain's cap at a jaunty angle, fiddling around with the donk, making sure everything is A-OK for his departure.

I smile, raise my glass of champagne, and wish him a safe journey.

*

Half of his ashes are placed in the plot beside Mum, with a bronze plaque reading: 'Gregory Patrick Carlson, Loved Husband and Father, At Rest 7.6.2004, 85 years old, "Together Again."' The remainder we keep until we can manage a family get-together at the St George Motor Boat Club.

Finally we gather at the water's edge to disperse what remains of Dad into Kogarah Bay, hopefully to settle among the boats at their moorings. The rain that has been falling lightly throughout the morning stops as if on cue. Trying to keep the occasion solemn, my brother, sister, and I say a few words – but as the urn is upended, a gust of wind from out of nowhere picks up the bloody ashes and blows them back at us, into our faces and onto our clothes. We're not sure if we should laugh or cry.

One could almost be tempted to believe that the old bastard deliberately conjured up that gust, and that wherever he is, he's saying 'Gotcha!' with a smirk on his face. Maybe it is his way of telling us to dust ourselves off and get on with our lives, something he was always urging each us to do.

*

For months after he'd gone, although not wracked with grief, I 'saw' him everywhere, and I think of him still. But although I was fortunate to have had the opportunity to reflect on our relationship and gain a new perspective on it, to be honest, I didn't experience any dramatic transformation. I am still much the same person, still my father's daughter, exhibiting the positive and negative traits we shared and still searching for that elusive 2 per cent. I can still hear him saying 'What are you, a complete dill?' and laughing.

Perhaps the only difference is that I can now laugh along with him.

Printed in the United States
By Bookmasters